bald in the land of big hair

bald in the land of big hair

a true story

Joni Rodgers

HarperCollins*Publishers*

HarperCollins books may be purchased for eductional, business, or sales promotional use. For information please write: Special Markets Department, HarperCollins Publishers Inc., 10 East 53rd Street, New York, NY 10022.

FIRST EDITION

Designed by Elina D. Nudelman

Library of Congress Cataloging-in-Publication Data
Rodgers, Joni.
    Bald in the land of big hair : a true story /
Joni Rodgers.
        p. cm.
    ISBN 0-06-019588-6
    1. Rodgers, Joni, —Health. 2. Lymphomas—
Patients—United States Biography. I. Title

    RC280.1'9699446'0092—dc21
    [B]   00-44984

01 02 03 04 05 RRD/❖ 10 9 8 7 6 5 4 3 2 1

THIS BOOK IS DEDICATED

To Sid, Wendy, Tracy, Melodie, Tonsi, and the many other brave women who've been there and done that.

TO THE MEMORY OF
Sarah, Violet, Sue, Theresa, Jackie, and the many other brave women whose journey took them still further.

And to Lagenia, still my lighthouse.

Contents

Acknowledgments and Forewarnings

The first lie of fiction is that the author gives some order to
the chaos of life: chronological order, or whatever order
the author chooses. As a writer, you select some part of a
whole; you decide that those things are important and the
rest is not. And you will write about those things from
your perspective. Life is not that way. Everything happens
simultaneously, in a chaotic way, and you don't make
choices. You are not the boss. Life is the boss.

ISABEL ALLENDE

*L*ife was the boss of this story. Some names have been
changed to protect the proverbial innocent, and several
events, characters, and conversations have been composited
for the sake of economy. Other than that, I felt compelled to
tell the chaotic truth—or at least my entirely biased version
of it. There's a traditional Kenyan prayer: "From the cowardice that dares not face new truth, from the laziness that is
content with half-truth, from the arrogance that thinks it
knows all truth, Good Lord, deliver me." That's been my
prayer every day I've worked on this book. To all the precious people who populate this story and bless my life, I
thank you for sharing my journey and beg your forgiveness
for any discomfort lurking in these pages.

Special thanks to my literary chick/chemo buds, Sidney
Burgess, Wendy Harpham, Lagenia Damron, and Debbie

Robertson, and to Fred Ramey for valued input and perspectives on early versions of the manuscript; to my agent, Laurie Harper, for believing in me in general and this project in particular; to my editor, Marjorie Braman, for her insightful guidance and good humor; and to Jeffery McGraw, long may he wave.

I'm enormously grateful to my oncologist, Dr. Jung-sil Ro, for her caring, candor, and vigilance; to her staff; and to all the medical folks who watch over my scans and blood samples. Thanks also to my race-walking partner and dear friend, Miss Gay Lynn Smallwood Pruitt, for dragging me out of bed every morning and making me be a healthier, happier person.

The love, music, and humor of my family has always been my lifeline: my gracious mother and dynamic father, Lois and Del Lonnquist; the Amazing Lonnquist Sisters, Linda, Diana, and Janis; my brothers, Allen and Roger; default sibs Pam, Ilidio, Michael, and Jan; and their inspiring assortment of offspring. (We miss you, Bruce.)

My son, Malachi, and daughter, Jerusha, keep me stocked up on pure joy, and when they read this book someday, I hope they'll see that my strength to survive grew largely out of my love for them.

Most of all, I want to thank my husband, best friend, and one great love, Gary Rodgers, who gives me a foundation to stand on, brings balance to all my craziness, and . . . well, like the song says, "There ain't nothin' like a brown-eyed handsome man."

—JR

bald in the land of big hair

BC (Before Cancer)

The butterfly sleeps well,
perched upon the temple bell . . .
Until it rings.

—BUSON

*W*hen tomorrow was still a given and ignorance was still bliss, I was floating along like a paper sailboat on a lazy river, too caught up in my life to know that I was dying. But the day you're diagnosed with cancer, you stop dying and start surviving. You stop living and start staying alive.

In that initial post-diagnosis pretreatment limbo read-everything-you-can-get-your-hands-on phase, I was desperate to learn the aggressive art of living, searching for anything that might give me a clue. Because, cancer-wise, I was clueless.

And I liked it that way.

Life was pretty darn good when I was dying. Before the *Titanic* hit the iceberg, before the flight attendant said, "Thank you for choosing Hindenberg Airlines," before the you-know-what hit the fan and Elvis left the building—right up until the day of my diagnosis, I was just "kickin' down the cobblestones, feelin' groovy." It's important to say that I was, on a fundamental level, happy.

I enjoyed an unconventional but idyllic childhood, the number-five child of two musicians who fell in love and had an octet. I grew up onstage, opening for various huge-haired country legends of the sixties at county fairs and small-town high school auditoriums. My father was a radio announcer, then manager, and eventually owner of a series of stations. Mom was the quintessential happy homemaker of the pre-Steinem era, giving guitar lessons or taking pictures and writing articles for the local newspaper on the side. The career she might have had in photojournalism during those years took a backseat to packing another U-Haul and setting up housekeeping in Wisconsin or Florida or Minnesota or Washington or wherever the residence du jour turned out to be.

"Was your dad in the military?" people often ask when I mention how much I moved around as a kid.

"Worse," I tell them. "He was in radio."

Mobility was a lesson I learned early. It endowed me with a fearlessness that comes from being familiar with unfamiliar surroundings. So at eighteen, confident I knew everything I would ever need to, I left home to seek adventure and forge my own diversified career in theater and broadcasting.

Gary and I met by serendipity and married by a Montana trout stream when I was twenty-one and he was thirty-one. Five years after that, I embarked on my second career: maternity leave. To everyone's surprise, including my own, I quit my full-time job in radio three months after my son, Malachi, was born, determined to be a mommy working, as opposed to a working mommy. It didn't start to sink in until two years later when my daughter, Jerusha, was born that by putting the mommy part first, I was relegating myself to a career composed of entrepreneurial fits and starts. Nonetheless, I became the quintessential happy homemaker of the *post*-Steinem era; an odd-job June Cleaver, solidly ensconced in a peaceful suburban existence, tempering motherhood with theatrical dabblings and an occasional voice-over gig (that was me on the Lipton Tea commercial, circa 1991, pointing out the difference between sippers and chuggers). As my theater contacts dwindled and my performance résumé thinned, I began to fill in by taking temporary office jobs when finances demanded.

One particular assignment I took as a part-time typist for an architectural firm lasted several months. The pay was good, the hours flexible, and child care accommodating. The office had fresh flowers every day, the people were as friendly as the up-to-date computers, and the windows looked out over picturesque downtown Bethlehem, Pennsylvania. But one day, as I stood in the elevator, watching the numbers tick upward to the tenth floor, I started to cry. Staring through blurry eyes at the mirrored interior of the elevator, I saw a woman in proper office attire, the only concession to individuality being a pair of funky cowboy boots.

That person was not me. This job was not what I wanted to do with my life.

Where was the adventure? Where was the art? Theater had always been my *biology*, but these days, the closest I came to directing was teaching a weekly creative drama class for preschoolers. The closest I came to acting was an occasional radio commercial extolling the virtues of Bob's Discount Tire Warehouse. When it bothered me, I cut my hair, ate a Reese's Peanut Butter Cup, did whatever little or big thing I had to do to feel better for the moment. Successfully avoiding effort, rejection, and the growing pains of self-discovery, I distracted myself with the superficial ding-dongs of daily existence—quacking telephone, shiny plastic, the self-imposed chore of making myself responsible for the wants and needs of everyone around me.

"The Zen genius," said Suzuki, "sleeps in every one of us and demands an awakening."

"What does a man profit," asked Jesus, "if he gains the whole world, but loses his soul?"

How many years, how much energy was I planning to spend denying my genius, neglecting my soul? I was already *thirtysomething*, for cryin' out loud. A grown-up by any calendar. Time to run with the big dogs or stay on the porch. I knew what I had to do before my last remaining spark of divine fire was irrevocably quenched. In a euphoric burst of liberating resolve, I stepped off the elevator, went into my boss's office, and quit.

"You did *wha*—?" Gary gulped, doing the mental math in spite of himself.

"I *had* to," I explained melodramatically. "Swallowing your destiny, ignoring what you were put on this planet to do—that's the kind of thing that eats you alive, Gary. That's the kind of thing that gives you *cancer*!" (Those glib little things we say. They have a way of coming back as gremlins to bite us on the backside, don't they?)

Six weeks later, I took a bold new stride toward my bold new destiny.

Now, I was a part-time typist for a development firm.

My *real* career was "on hold" until my kids were in school, I told myself, and I tried not to think about the way my mother's talents were still simmering on that back burner long after her children had grown up and gone.

But not to worry, I figured. I had plenty of time.

*T*hat winter, I turned thirty-one. Gary traced growing handprints inside a homemade birthday card. He closed his big hand around Jerusha's tiny fist and helped her write "Rudy" next to hers, and Malachi scrawled "Ike" next to his all by himself. Admonishing me to keep my eyes closed, they led me blindman's-bluff style into the kitchen.

"Ta-da!" Gary baritoned, backed up by preschool squeals of delight.

"A computer!" I thrilled until my practical self kicked in. "Can we afford it?"

"No," Gary said, "but you've always talked about wanting to write, and . . . well, you're not really working now. Just staying home with the kids for the most part."

Not really working? My heart always sank when he made comments like that. I've waited tables and worked on assembly lines. I've toured eight shows a week and pulled twelve-hour air shifts, but I've never worked as hard in my life as I did "just staying home with the kids." I could have easily launched into my usual "anyone who gets bored being a stay-at-home parent isn't doing it right" diatribe, but disarmed by his goofy grin, I looked inside the card instead.

"Happy Birthday," he'd written. "This is to show I know your brain hasn't turned to Wheatina."

It felt like he was showing me a snapshot of someone I used to be; recognizing how much of myself I'd given to motherhood since the kids came along and reminding me the person I was before they came along might still exist, slumbering under a layer of Similac and sandbox grit.

I soon discovered I could type, rock Jerusha on my lap, and play Hi Ho! Cherry-O with Malachi, all at the same time. The first draft of my first novel began to take shape.

I stayed up late into the night, waled on it during "Reading Rainbow" and "Zoobilee Zoo" and any other block of hours or minutes I could put together. The characters emerged and made themselves known to me, and I went with them like a hitchhiker, hoping they'd ultimately go in my general direction: and we all just kept going together until it felt like a journey. Like a full circle. Like a book.

The following autumn, I was invited to direct a play I loved at a theater where I'd enjoyed working as an actor in two past productions. The timing seemed right. Malachi was in first grade, and Jerusha was yearning to ride that big yellow bus, so I enrolled her in preschool and enthusiastically accepted the job.

This script was collected from the Wakefield Cycles and other sacred artifacts of pre-Shakespearean theatre and included some lovely, lively old dances, which I dutifully learned alongside my cast. The choreographer was cranky but brilliant, and I chalked it up to her rigorous rehearsals when I discovered—to my delight—that I was losing weight. For the first and only time in my life, I could eat anything I wanted. A gift from God! And perfect timing, because I was also experiencing an insatiable craving for anything chocolate. The stress, I told myself, unwrapping another candy bar, and as the stress mounted, Baby Ruth, Mr. Goodbar, and the Three Musketeers became my new best buddies.

I loved this play. I kept reminding myself how much I loved it as I slogged through a tremendous amount of research; sorted a nightmarish array of sixteenth-century props, costumes, and musical instruments; and schmoozed a leading man whose self-absorbed Stanislovsky methodology somehow didn't include learning his lines. I coddled and cajoled, struggling to maintain my maternal directing style, but on opening night, I sat in the dark of the theater with clenched stomach, constricted lungs, and burning eyes as he mangled the script I held in such reverence. Studies have shown increased free radicals in the bloodstream in response to anger and anxiety, and now that I think of it, it did feel like poison. By the end of the production, the boundless energy with which I'd begun had dwindled to a deep desire to hibernate for the rest of the winter.

The play closed on New Year's Eve, and I turned thirty-two four weeks later. Through February and March, it seemed to snow endlessly, and I blamed the weather for an indefinable, vaguely oppressive smog that settled over me even as spring came on.

Looking back, I can pinpoint the night before Easter as the last innocent evening of my lovely, oblivious life BC. I remember setting out Easter baskets for Gary, Malachi, and Jerusha. I didn't make one for myself (martyrdom being a job requirement for both mothers and Easter bunnies), but I scavenged chocolate from everyone else's as I decorated them with curly ribbon and colored eggs. After my customary half hour on the weight machine, half hour on the stepper, I drank my customary cup of chamomile tea and went to bed.

Sunday morning, when I tried to get up, I couldn't stand. The pain in my back was so intense, I could barely feel my legs. An ambulance whisked me to the hospital, where someone in scrubs pumped me full of morphine and steroids, and technicians took a CAT scan from the bottom of my tailbone to the top of my shoulder blades. If they'd gone just a few inches higher, they might have seen the small lump that was beginning to press on nerves in my neck.

Three hazy days later, they told me they needed the room for somebody else, and feeling better, I was eager for them to give it to her. Readily accepting the ambiguous diagnosis of "disc problems," I allowed Gary to take me home and tuck me in with a heating pad, painkillers, and another dose of steroids. That afternoon, he told me as gently as he could that the airline was closing their Allentown-Bethlehem maintenance base, giving him the choice of being laid off or transferred to Houston, Texas.

"Wooo . . . ," I slurred. "Luckily, I'm so tanked right now, I can't even comprehend what you're saying to me."

Moving occupied both my brain power and waking hours for the major part of the summer, but somewhere in the midst of the packing and the purging and the yard sale and the disconnect notices, I went to the nearest HMO doctor, a tiny Filipino man who had an office on one side of his rambling Edwardian row house. I told him that my energy was down, my forearms were itchy, and I couldn't shake that craving for chocolate.

He thumped my knee with a hammer and told me it sounded like PMS. But when he took my temperature, it was slightly elevated. I told him I seemed to be running a low-grade fever like that almost every night.

"What's wrong with me?" I asked as he peered into my ear with a flashlight.

"You sick," he nodded conclusively.

I left his office with a prescription for penicillin and the directive to "take it easy," a tall Rx considering the yard-long list of things I had to do before our impending departure.

We waved good-bye to Pennsylvania, Gary at the wheel of an enormous Ryder-Penske truck, me following in the family car with the kids in the backseat, singing "This is the song that never ends" all the way to Texarkana. By the time we arrived in Houston, we were exhausted and hot, but happy to be home.

We spent the Fourth of July in Galveston, walked down the beach toward a spectacular sunset, then sat along the seawall, salt air stinging our noses, fireworks lighting up our eyes along with the sky above and the Gulf of Mexico below. Gary put his arms around me, and I leaned into him.

"I think we're really going to love it here," I said.

And he said, "Yup. This is going to be a great year."

Treachery.

On a cellular level, my body must have known our best-laid plans were about to go awry, but instead of telling me, it allowed me to blather on, business as usual. It lent me a thin veneer of acceptably functional health while plotting a silent suicide pact with the twisted cells that snickered and mutated and multiplied like termites.

It makes me think of the insecticide commercials where the roaches are having a big ol' party until the can of Raid appears. My cells were having a big ol' party, all right. They'd turned my lymph nodes into brothels and pool halls and Casino Royales. Tiny-tassled bimbo cells were jumping out of cakes and lap dancing for beer-bellied, cigar-smoking lymphocytes who tucked dollar bills into garter belts around their nuclei. Back-alley bad-boy cells were rolling dice and running games on innocent passersby. Pin-striped thug cells were shaking down shop owners and slipping Mickeys to my immune system.

And not a can of Raid in sight.

1

Lunch at the Premonition Café

Men argue. Nature acts.
—VOLTAIRE

*R*ight off, I discovered the best way to handle the heat of a Houston summer: go to Montana.

Helena is the closest thing I've ever had to a hometown. I wasn't born there, but my children were, and my parents still lived there, along with my big sister and her family and my little brother and his wife. I'd lived there more than I'd ever lived anywhere else and couldn't bear to be away from the mountains for more than twelve months at a stretch. Fortunately, I was able to finance a trip home every year by returning to my old summer job at Grandstreet Theatre, where I taught kindergarten, first-, and second-grade creative drama classes. For two weeks every year, I played the Whoosh-Whoosh game and led my merry little band of jumping beans on imaginary journeys through jungles and dragonlands and mysterious kingdoms where you could become a different person just by changing your hat. (Nice work, if you can get it.)

But this summer, my whoosh-whoosh energy was a little low. After class the first day, I went home and crashed on the couch at my parents' house. When my mom came home from work a little while later, she settled an afghan over me and laid her hand on my forehead for a moment. I'm well acquainted with that universal gesture of motherly concern (the palm of my hand, I like to brag, is accurate to within a tenth of a degree).

I knew I should open my eyes and tell her I was fine, but it was such a lovely feeling. Being tucked in. Being a child instead of a mommy, just for that brief instant. So I lay there pretending, feeling a little guilty but mostly grateful for a modicum of that mama-bear nurturing no one ever gets enough of. Unless they're sick.

Of course, I know anyone you slept with before you slept with your spouse is supposed to be anathema, canceled like a bad check that returns to you stamped *NSF* for Non-Sufficient . . . um . . . Fellowship. You are to tear this relationship in two, pay the penalty, and never think of it again except in shame and regret.

My folks never approved of Jon, and truth be told, I lie awake contemplating how I'll prevent my own daughter from ever getting involved in such an affair. I was a twenty-year-old disc jockey. He was about forty, stood four inches shorter than I, and introduced me to orgasms, antisocialism, and acid. The relationship had had such a profound effect on my life, it was almost unbearable to realize I was barely a blip on his radar screen. For years, the sting of it was such that I wouldn't speak his name. On the rare occasions I did allow his memory to intrude on my consciousness or my conversations, I referred to him only as "the gimlet."

I honestly thought he was out of my system, but when I sat down during "Reading Rainbow" to write my first novel, it accidentally turned out to be the story of a young disc jockey (me) who falls in love with an aging rancher (gimlet). The original outline ended in humiliation and death for the old sod. But somehow, as the story told itself to me and I told it to the keyboard, the fairy-tale characters performed reconstructive surgery on true life. The fictional man convinced me to forgive the real thing, and the fictional girl reminded me that I didn't love Jon because I was an idiot. I loved him because he was, and is, a remarkable person.

"Call me later," he said the day he broke my heart, "just so I know we're cool."

I'm fairly certain he didn't mean *twelve years* later, but I decided to call, anyway, to ask his forgiveness and offer mine. We ended up talking for hours, and by the time we hung up, we were cool. Old flames smoldered down to old friends. I sent Jon a copy of the manuscript he'd helped inspire, and we agreed to meet for lunch while I was in Helena.

Montana was sunny and arid and Russel Chatham–watercolor beautiful that day, as it is most days in high July. The theater-school session was almost over. The children and I were putting the finishing touches on our musical adaptation of *Where the Wild Things Are*. After class, I helped them gather their magic carpet squares, construction paper Hobblegobs, and other take-home items, dispensing Tootsie Pops and good-bye hugs as I shooed them out the door.

Slumped in a booth at Bert 'n' Ernie's half an hour later, frowzled by a full morning of Quacknoodles and papier-mâché, I waited for Jon to mosey in with his long ponytail and funky attire reflecting his Native American blood and a sturdy tradition of too much sun, country music, and alcohol. But time and miles were beginning to show on him; his hair was cropped to a respectable collar-length, and the crinkles that used to be only for laughing were now set in stone. He'd taken an early retirement. He was sick. Some kind of heart problem.

"Hi there," he said warmly, and I wasn't sure if I should get up and hug him, so I just said, "Hi there also."

"Well." He laid my manuscript on the table and sat down. "I didn't know you had it in you."

"You think it stinks," I instantly concluded. "You hate it." I regretted showing it to him. He was intimidatingly well-read, and I was still feeling fragile about my words.

"No! I didn't hate it at all."

"It's just a rough draft. Rough drafts are allowed to stink horrendously."

"It doesn't stink."

"It stinks. You can be honest. Go ahead. Be brutally honest."

"It doesn't stink! Your spelling stinks. The rest is good. It's really . . . good. I stayed up all night reading it. And I tried to call you at the theater, because I wanted you to know, but then I had to walk around with all this . . . knowing, and I just wanted to tell you . . . I liked it. A lot."

The waiter came, and I wondered if I shouldn't clarify that we were just friends, that I had a husband in Houston who was way taller than this guy. Instead, we ordered taco salads and beer and embarked on the standard catching-up conversation.

"So how long are you here?" Jon asked.

"Another ten days or so." Rocky Mountain vacations tend to be sort of free-form for us. "Gary's coming to see my students perform this weekend, then we might go fishing over in Livingston or take the kids to Yellowstone or whatever."

"Always lots of whatever to do around Montana."

"Yup," I agreed. "And for some reason, Montana makes me do things I wouldn't do anywhere else."

"Like what?"

"Oh, ride horses . . . wear a hat . . . get a tattoo."

"You didn't."

I giggled like a sophomore, and Jon didn't bother to pretend he wasn't curious.

"What sort of artwork are we talking about here?"

"Oh, it's so pretty! It's a pink rosebud with leaves and tendrils that curve up around . . . well, around a blossoming rose—only that rose is . . . what was already there."

He didn't get it.

"*There*," I repeated, indicating my left nipple.

"Ah." He absorbed that for a moment, then winced. "Sounds painful."

"Excruciating." I nodded proudly. "But I happen to have a very high threshold."

"What was Gary's reaction?"

"It's going to be a surprise."

"I'll bet."

"He'll like it." I was confident, having elaborately planned the delicious moment of unveiling and primed Gary for it by mailing a series of erotically charged letters.

"What in the world made you go and get a tattoo?"

"Well, for one thing, I've always hated myself there because I'm so flat chested—but now, I'm beautiful there! *Finally*." I spared him the analogy supplied by the tatoo artist: if you can't grow melons, plant roses. "And I guess . . . well, I just want to shake Gary up a little, you know? Let him know that somewhere, under all these years of floor scrubbing and diaper changing, I'm still the rowdy girl he fell in love with." I hated how it sounded like I was defending a lukewarm marriage, so I dug into my backpack for a new topic. "So you want to see pictures?"

Jon drew back and wrinkled his forehead.

"Of my kids."

"Oh! Yeah. Sure," he nodded out of politeness (or relief), and I whipped out my plastic accordion of photos.

"Here's Malachi. We call him 'Ike.' He just turned seven, and he's already read *Jurassic Park*. Not a kid's version. The real book by Michael Crichton, I'm not kidding. We told him we'd only take him to the movie if he read the book first. And here's Jerusha. 'Rudy' for short. And she's turning out so smart and brave and funny. And so beautiful."

"Not terribly surprising." Jon slid the snapshots back across the table, and I dragged them noisily into my purse, trying to duck the compliment.

"So . . . that's the kids," I said. "Ike 'n' Rudy. Getting big."

"So they are."

"Rudy starts kindergarten this fall. It feels kind of . . . empty nest."

"What will you do with yourself all day?"

"Well, Gary just got transferred to Houston, which is a big market. Lots of theater going on. If I can get a good talent agent, I'll be able to fill in between shows with voice-overs. And I know it sounds crazy, and I know there's a lot of work to do on it, and it's next to impossible and everything— but I want to see if I can find a publisher for this book. If I don't, Jon, it's going to burn a hole in my liver."

"What about radio?" Jon asked. His first glimpse of me was over the airwaves, so in his mind, I'll always belong there.

"I don't want to get locked into anything inflexible. It's better if I stay project oriented."

"That's a nice way of saying 'dilettante,' isn't it?"

"Ha-ha. I know it's not the greatest way to make money, but it lets me keep my focus mainly on the mommy thing. And I have an idea for another novel."

"Uh-oh. Will I be in that one, too?"

"Don't flatter yourself," I pointed at him with my salad fork. "You were a one-book fling, and even that required some heavy-duty creative writing."

"So what's it about?"

"What would have happened if Eros and Psyche had been southeast Texas trailer trash instead of a Greek god and goddess."

He raised his eyebrows but reserved comment.

"If I know you," he predicted, "you'll be pregnant before the year is out."

"Then you don't know me," I bristled. "I had my tubes tied five years ago."

"Fran did, too." Something changed in his eyes. "She had a miscarriage. And then they discovered cancer."

"Oh . . . no . . ."

I could see in his face how much it had terrified him. I reached around my heart for whatever it is you're supposed to say in a case like that, but I didn't know how to respond to a topic I found so altogether . . . *ooky.*

"So . . . is she okay?" I asked. "Did she do the . . . the . . . treatment?"

"No, just the surgery, and now they watch."

"You guys have had a tough year."

Jon just nodded and tipped his beer.

"It's good that you have each other."

He probably didn't need to be reminded, but this was his severalth marriage, and I was still connected to the local grapevine enough to know this woman was the best thing that ever happened to him. I worried like a nanny he was going to go and screw it up somehow, but it would be even worse if he finally found a wife he could stick with, only to have her up and die of cancer.

"Have you seen Sid?" he asked, as though mention of the C-word had brought the specter of our mutual friend into the room, pale, thin, turbaned, and pathetically brave in what we all assumed was her eleventh hour.

"I know I should call her," I answered. "But I never know what to say. How is she?"

"Looks like it's beating up on her pretty good."

"That whole chemotherapy thing is so barbaric. I don't know how she can do that to herself," I shuddered (sending forth another one of those glib little gremlins). "I'd never do that. I'd do surgery and natural medicine. Herbs and stuff. But if that didn't work, I would accept that nature had selected me for extinction and go gracefully."

Jon looked at me as if I'd walked under a ladder, kicked a black cat, and shouted "Macbeth" backstage in a crowded theater.

"Let's hope you never have to test that theory," he said in benediction.

I stirred at my salad, and we talked about how Helena had changed, what with that new Wal-Mart coming to town, and how it was for him in the hospital with his heart, and other gossip and news of home and folks. Then Jon started singing some Willie Nelson song, the lyrics of which were pertinent to some point he was making about a particular part of my novel that had made him laugh.

I should remember that song, I keep thinking now.

The lyrics should have seared into my mind with sirens and alarms and *Psycho* violins. But all I remember is resting my chin in my hand as I listened to Jon's relaxed tenor. I didn't realize I was stroking my neck until he stopped and said, "Sore throat?"

"No, just . . . I guess my glands are kind of swollen."

"You must be coming down with something. Feel okay?"

"I've been really tired lately, but—you know," I brushed it away so it wouldn't sound like whining. "The altitude and theatre school and moving and everything."

"You need vitamin C," was his diagnosis. Like all sick people, he was suddenly an expert on health.

We talked a little more on our way to the cashier's podium, where we exchanged a comfortably chaste hug.

"You know," I said, "the way it worked out—it's kind of like the book. There was a happy ending. Just not with each other."

"Don't forget your vitamins," he smiled.

"You either," I said, and stepped out into the blinding mountain sunlight.

I went back to Houston, and the Lump went with me.

The Lump, later called the Mass, later called the Suspicious Mass, later called the Cancer. Forming in the primordial soup of my lymphatic system, it slithered forth like some Precambrian tadpole, grew legs, became aggressive, intelligent, predatory; evolving from a nagging intuition to a great barking bullfrog that wouldn't let me sleep nights.

Dr. Bernie Siegel might make something of the fact that it seized me by the throat. I had started singing onstage at age three, made my adult living with my voice, loved to drink, lived to eat, gave good head and even better phone. Dr. Andrew Weil might point to the dietary habits of a confessed carnivore and sugar fiend. A scientist might tell me it all originated in a glitched, recessive gene or a whiff of toxic environment, a red dye number two licorice whip, or the same diet cola that killed experimental rats but was peddled by fabulously streamlined models to a culture full of people who would walk naked into a nuclear reactor if they thought it would melt cellulite. Or maybe the metaphysicians are right about a soul's yearning for the astral plane. My mother believes God was trying to tell me something, but if she thought I was being punished for doing lunch with my old lover, she never said so. And for that, I'm grateful.

Maybe my body figured it was payback time for all the Slim-Fast migraines and Little Debbie binges, for too much Boone's Farm apple wine on the dormitory roof and not enough sleep between the late show and the alarm clock, for all the years of great expectation and nonappreciation, for forgetting that every human body is a temple and that this body in particular was the habitat of my own blithe spirit. Perhaps it was rooted in a deep subconscious desire to be the center of attention, to lie around in front of the TV, or to take a break from shaving my underarms. *Maybe*—I've accused myself in my most irrational moments of guilt and shame— maybe, I secretly *wanted* to have cancer. Perhaps, if I were better and stronger and had more faith, instead of being the deeply flawed, pudgy-thighed failure that I was, none of this would have happened.

But in more lucid moments, I recognize that the incidence of non-Hodgkin's lymphoma has doubled since I was in high school. In 1994, I was one of about fifty thousand people diagnosed, and half of us did not live to see the new century. In 2000, more than 62,000 people were told they had lymphoma, even as the overall cancer rate continued a steady decline. It's undeniable that something in our environment is causing young women to contract a virulent strain of this disease once seen almost exclusively in elderly men, but we don't know what that something is, and to my knowledge, very little is being done to find out. Probably because we, as a society, don't want to know what it is any more than I, as an individual, wanted to awaken to the truth of what was happening to me.

"What's the use of wonderin'?" the Rodgers and Hammerstein soprano used to warble, but I do wonder. Not *why me?* but *how?* and *when?*

And *what else?*

All I know for certain is there was a carcinogen, there was a climate, and somehow, a tiny part of me mutinied.

I envy my husband. He has an explanation that satisfies him completely.

"Shit happens," Gary shrugs, quoting some pithy T-shirt philosopher of yore, and that is apt phraseology. Because in the great barnyard of life, cancer is a manure pile. It stinks, but it makes great fertilizer.

2

Cleopatra, Queen of Denial

Pain is the price you pay for
resisting life.

—DR. PHIL MCGRAW

$\mathcal{B}$ack in Houston, I unpacked boxes, enrolled the
kids at their new school, and started learning my way around
town; how to get to the grocery store, the nearest movie theater, the doctor's office.

When I took the kids in for their school-year checkups, I
mentioned to the GP my waning energy, the itchiness on my
forearms, the swollen glands, low-grade fevers, and unusual
craving for chocolate. He said it sounded like PMS, but also
suggested I change my brand of laundry soap. Then he prescribed antibiotics, though he couldn't actually see anything
wrong. I went in on another occasion because my back was
still bothering me, but again, I happily buried the symptoms
in Decadron, putting my concerns on hold until school
started in the fall. School started, and I put my concerns on
hold while I looked for a talent agent. I signed with a talent

agency, then put my concerns on hold while I auditioned for commercials and made the résumé rounds, schlepping my demo tape to every ad agency and theatre in town.

Now it was autumn, and I was standing in the bathroom, pulling my hair into a French braid. I twisted an extra notch in the binding and cleared several wavy auburn strands from the sink. My thick braid wasn't quite as long or as heavy as it used to be. Blaming stress, different water, and the new climate, I'd slathered on expensive conditioners. When that didn't work, I'd had a couple of inches trimmed off the end, then another inch, then three inches. Nothing seemed to help.

"Geez," Gary observed helpfully, "you've been shedding like an Irish setter."

"Thanks for noticing," I groused.

"Any time." He stepped close behind me, his hands roving under my shirt, tracing the tendrils around the rose, kissing his way from my shoulder to my neck until his soft whiskers tickled just below my right jaw.

"Hey." He suddenly drew away and tipped my head gently to the side. "What the hell is that?"

Not the words a woman longs to hear while having her neck nibbled by the man she adores. Still, there were no psycho strings or sirens.

But Gary told me later, "That was the moment I knew you had cancer."

Gary insisted I go immediately to another doctor, who was actually a nurse practitioner, managed care's answer to hypochondriacs and other people who are probably just whining. By now, I was so tired, I couldn't seem to make it through the day. Malachi and Jerusha would arrive home from school and find me napping on the couch. I was beginning to have difficulty swallowing, and the chocolate cravings intensified and expanded to include foods I otherwise never ate: bacon-double-cheeseburgers, french fries, sickening amounts of hot fudge. After I put on about five pounds, I squashed the cravings with Dexatrim, forced myself to stick to a strict diet, and tried to work out as often as I could, but I was still packing on about a pound per week. My initial unexplainable weight loss was a far more typical early symptom of non-Hodgkins lymphoma, but a nutritionist told me later that the subsequent weight gain was a sign that my metabolism was shutting down. It also contributed to a general feeling of *otherness* I couldn't really describe and so never mentioned to the nurse practitioner.

I was convinced I had mononucleosis, but when initial blood tests turned up nothing, I was given another round of antibiotics and an invitation to call back if the lump didn't disappear in a few weeks. It didn't. I called back and was graduated to a real doctor.

"I just don't feel like myself," I tried to explain. "I don't feel that bad really, just . . . weird. And my husband says my glands are swollen," I added, so he'd know I wasn't just whining.

Another battery of tests confirmed my worst fear: I *was* just whining.

He told me there was nothing wrong with me, but dispensed some innocuous cough syrup, anyway, along with the usual shotgun spray of antibiotics. When I pointed out that none of this had done me any good so far, he handed me a pamphlet about stress, made more dismissive references to PMS, and invited me to give him a call if the lump didn't go away in eight or ten weeks.

"Bullshit," Gary said when I told him. And he got that testosterone-powered–lawn mower look you sometimes see on the larger primates. "You're not waiting."

He called the doctor and got nowhere, called the nurse practitioner and berated, bellowed, and begged for another referral, suggesting that maybe the doctor had made a *mistake* and other blasphemies. I stood beside the phone, coaching him to be polite, fluttering, apologizing, feeling like a mouse in the White House. Gary seemed to take the unthinkable attitude that just because he paid these people to render a service, that gave him the right to assert his *opinion* or something. He reminded the nurse practitioner that almost ten weeks had passed since the date of my first appointment, over three months since I'd first noticed the swelling beneath my jawline, and she finally wrangled me a referral to an otolaryngologist. (That's what an ear, nose, and throat doctor calls himself when he's trying to pick up chicks.) I called the office, explained my situation, and was given an appointment almost six weeks down the road.

"No," said Lawn Mower Man. "You need to go now."

"Geez!" I said. "You are really beginning to irk me. Would you stop being such an alarmist?"

He wouldn't. He called the otolaryngologist's office repeatedly in an attempt to get them to move the appointment up. Two weeks later they had a cancellation and couldn't wait to get him off their collective back.

"Probably an infection of some sort," the kindly old Dr. K. assured me. "We'll give you a two-week course of antibiotics and run some tests."

As the tests continued coming back negative, Dr. K.—unbeknownst to me—began to do battle with my insurance company. He wanted to do a biopsy immediately, but it seems Gary and I were enrolled in a Christian Scientist HMO; apparently, any form of medical intervention was against their religion. Repeated requests for the biopsy never made it past the desk of the HMO bean counter, who was about as qualified as Chucklenuts the Clown to be making medical decisions on my behalf but nevertheless felt ol' Dr. K. was getting too many negative results lately with his *better-safe-than-sorry* approach. "Hey, sum o' them bah-opseez shouldn'ta bin dun!" he figgered. "Them things cost *money*, gol durn it!" Much better to forgo that vital early diagnosis and take a crapshoot with my life. These are, after all, the same fine folks who thought up the concept of outpatient mastectomies (my friend Theresa used to call that the Crash Slash). Criminy. At least Chucklenuts can make balloon animals.

Frustrated, Dr. K. ordered another pointless round of blood tests, and we waited two more weeks. By my next appointment, the lump was palpably larger, and on the struggle-to-stay-upright scale, my energy level had nose-dived from "kinda nappy" to "post–Grateful Dead concert."

"I have to make a phone call," Dr. K. said grimly. He came back forty-five minutes later to talk about the biopsy to be done in ten days.

Now, I must confess, I was getting a little nervous. *Biopsy* is one of those terms that snags on the back of the mind—like *IRS* or *subpoena*.

Still, there was no outright panic yet. No one had actually mentioned the word *cancer*. Dr. K., a gracious southern gentleman whose deep, sycamore voice made everything sound nonthreatening, used the word *lymphoma* once or twice, but I had no idea what that was. None of the professional people I'd been dealing with appeared to be anxious, and their apathy was more contagious than Ebola. After months of being shuffled here and there by a parade of comfortably unconcerned medical folk, I remained snuggled in a blanket of false security. And rightly so. To feel swollen glands and immediately scream, "Cancer!" would be a hysterical reaction. My friend Wendy Harpham, a doctor and writer who's also had cancer, once explained to me, "Doctors learn in medical school that when they hear hoofbeats, they should think 'horses,' not 'zebras.'"

However, there's anecdotal evidence abounding of women who were diagnosed long after they might have been, primarily because a woman who expresses too much concern about herself is dismissed as a whiner.

Another friend of mine, who'd had thyroid cancer shortly after the birth of her first child, detected a lump in her breast shortly after the birth of her second. Shannon's doctor dismissed her concerns, saying it was a cyst and her fears were an emotional reaction to the memory of her prior cancer experience. Months went by as she and her husband agonized, pleading with her physician to do a biopsy, begging her insurance company to authorize it, and ultimately paying out of their own pocket to have the damn thing done. Shannon was diagnosed with inflammatory breast cancer, an especially swift and devastating disease that has a terrifyingly low survival rate, especially when not detected immediately. She then had to turn around and battle these same people who now refused to authorize her bone marrow transplant (BMT), saying since she was so far gone, her probability of survival was not sufficient to justify the expense. After months of legal cockfighting, the procedure was approved, but by then, the cancer had gone to Shannon's bones. The BMT bought her some time, but she died shortly before her daughter's third birthday.

There are far too many cases like Shannon's, partly because many of us are easily dismissed and sometimes even intimidated by our doctors, partly because many of us have been taught to dismiss ourselves. "How are you?" they would ask, and I'd mention the fatigue, but then rush to add,

"Of course, I'm tired, though! Blah, blah two kids . . . blah, blah moving . . . blah, blah job hunting . . . blah, blah trying to lose ten pounds." I can't look back and feel angry at these people for ignoring my questions. I didn't ask any! Long before I was a distant *lub-dub* in their chilly stethoscopes, I'd learned that mommies are supposed to be exhausted all the time, and they aren't supposed to bitch about it to people who actually have lives. I willingly accepted the nondiagnoses and took the steroids and the painkillers and antibiotics, wishing the whole thing would just disappear.

"This is going to be nothing," I said, pulling on plain gray sweats in the plain gray predawn of Biopsy Day. "And I'll have a big hacking scar on my neck."

"So what?" Gary grimly pulled his own sweats on. They were black. Ninja Surgery Chauffeur.

"So I'm not going," I told him.

"The hell you're not."

Am not.

Are too.

Am not.

Are too.

Usually our arguments are a lot more stimulating than this, popping with sexual chemistry, rife with witty Noel Coward repartee. (At the climax of one particular tempest, I actually ate a JCPenney charge card receipt just to show him I was *not* going to return a pair of purple shoes.) But my heart wasn't in this one. I knew he was right. It wasn't nothing. Once you say the word *biopsy*, you've passed out of the nothing realm into something territory, whether that something is malignant or benign.

"Life can only be understood backward," said Soren Kierkegaard, "but it must be lived forward."

As I stood in the surgical center elevator, watching the

numbers tick upward to the twelfth floor, I started to cry. There was nowhere to hide now, no leaving town, no marching into the boss's office to quit. After I was prepped for surgery, I lay waiting for the anesthesiologist. I wished she would hurry. I was eager to be unconscious.

But just on the other side of my pounding heart, I was amazed to find a strange exhilaration. Something had been telling me since that day in the architect's office I needed to change direction, and now I would. Something had been slowly but surely taking my life away from me, and now I would at least be able to call it by its name.

Cancer was not the first time I went to war with myself.

Every fitting-room session was a battle, as was every crampy menstrual period, every saggy-eyed morning in the mirror. From the time I was sixteen, I, like most women I know, was in conflict with my body. I apologized for it, jokingly at auditions, earnestly at photo sessions, shyly as I gave it for the first time to a slightly geeky, sweetly bookish boy on the top bunk in his post-Salinger dorm room. As if a flat chest and broad thighs weren't bad enough, childbirth and time added thick ankles and stretch marks to the indictment. And I never did like my nose, and my hair. . . . Well, let's not even go there.

But I never actually used the word *gargoyle* until I stared into the mirror at my blotchy post-surgery complexion, bloating above the gruesome biopsy scar. A four-inch chain of black stitches secured angry red edges, underscoring a misshapen gullet and giving the impression of a detachable head.

"My bride!" Gary teased, stalking me with his arms outstretched stiff like Mary Shelley's monster. "Gloria Frankensteinem!"

I faced my fate with an unwavering courage and . . . well, OK—with a relatively small amount of cowardice and . . . oh, all right—with *drugs!* Good drugs! The expensive kind! And lots of 'em! Praise God and pass the Valium.

Maybe that accounted for my Waldenesque post-biopsy introspection. Whatever the catalyst, it did seem that in the days following the diagnosis, the noise of every day began to fall quiet around me. Momentum that had always carried me forward like a freight train rolled to a halt. What had seemed the most pressing obligations were now the least significant, and I couldn't help but see the parallel between my denial of the long overdue changes needed in my life and my denial of the cancer that had already seeped from one small lymph node, to both sides of my neck and down toward my chest.

I'd always given away my time and efforts as easily as an old lady offers knickknacks at a yard sale, asking little and accepting even less. From Bunk Boy to bosses to the PTO volunteer coordinator, no one ever had to beg for their piece of me, and not recognizing that all those little pieces added up to my life, I performed in overdrive to make sure I surpassed their expectations. Now, for the first time in my life, *my life* was at the top of my agenda.

Women of my generation don't know what to do with that. We've grown accustomed to the idea that we should be doing the work of at least two people, and we've learned to pacify ourselves and others while our sleeping spirit slumbers on. But sooner or later, the alarm goes off. We're forced to open our eyes. And much to our surprise, there is light.

3

Lights, Cancer, Action

Just say the lines.

—BETTE DAVIS

(*M*erengue theme music, bongo drums up and under)

ANNOUNCER: It's "I Love Lymphy!" Starring the Cancer Woman and the Cancer Woman's husband!

(Gary enters)

GARY: Honey, I'm home!

JONI: (Rushes out to kiss him in her fluffy crinolines and impeccable housedress.) Hi, honey! How was your night?

GARY: Hey! Is that a casaba melon in your neck or are you just happy to see me? (Audience laughter.)

JONI: Oh, my glands have been a little swollen.

GARY: I've heard of having a lump in your throat, but this is ridiculous! (More laughs.) Let's get you to a doctor! (Cut to doctor's office, where Joni and Gary sit facing Doctor wearing Groucho glasses and mustache.)

GARY: So, Doc, will she ever play the violin again?

DOCTOR: Did she play before?

GARY: No, but she's very high-strung. (Laughter.)

JONI: All right, just cut to the chase. What's wrong with me?

DOCTOR: Testing indicates *clankankorous miss moss pooniak slar.*

JONI and GARY: Huh?

DOCTOR: *Blah reeb moo noo spahsh mlork* malignant *plasnurtion.*

GARY and JONI: Huh?

DOCTOR: *Sporken melzer* disease *foo obner* non-Hodgkin's lymphoma.

JONI: What's that?

GARY: You know—Hodgkins. Those little guys in the Wizard of Oz.

DOCTOR: . . . *splee fwink snavel popper* lymphatic system.

JONI: Does that mean it's . . .

DOCTOR: *Woop woop dee jarmud* oncologist immediately *plinka meesh meesh* chemotherapy. *Quarp nermop kabibulous* life-threatening condition.

JONI: But is it—is it— (Leaps up and grabs him by the front of his lab coat.) Just say the word, will you? Say it, say it, *say it,* for God's sake!

DOCTOR: What's the matter? Don't you people speak English?! (He takes out a large rubber stamp and plants "CANCER" in large red letters across Joni's forehead.)

JONI: *Waaaaaaaaaaaaaaaaaahhhhhhhhhhh!*

(Cut to library. Joni and Gary are sitting at a table. Canned laughter as librarian hefts a few more thick and intimidating tomes on top of a pile several feet high.)

JONI: I have cancer.

LIBRARIAN: Alrighty, then you'll want something inspirational. We just got the latest in this series: *Chicken Soup for the Condemned to Hell Soul.* Or how about this one: *Don't Sweat the Small Stuff—and It's All Small Stuff Except for Cancer, Which is Godzilla.*

GARY: Actually, we're looking for some hard information.

LIBRARIAN: Let's see. There should be something in *The Illustrated Encyclopedia of Doom and Despair.*

GARY: Yes, here we are. "Non-Hodgkin's Lymphoma . . . cancer of the lymphatic system . . . see also 'hideous scourge of the reaper.'"

JONI: Oh my Lord!

GARY: Just kidding! Ha-ha-ho. Just havin' a little fun with ya, honey.

JONI: (Seizes book and bashes him over the head with it.) Knock that off and tell me what it really says.

GARY: Hmmm. Says here the prognosis is generally—wooo Nelly! Umm . . . er . . . well, this thing is obviously defective. Let's try something else.

LIBRARIAN: Here we go! *The Lipschitz Anthology of Gross Deformities and Devastating Diseases.*

GARY: "Untreated, high grade non-Hodgkin's lymphoma is fatal within six to twelve months." How long did you say you've had that lump, honey?

JONI: About seven months.

GARY: (To the pretty librarian) So what are you doing New Year's Eve? (Joni whacks him with the book again.) Ouch! Okay! Okay! Let's try this one. *Death for Dummies.* Yes, here it is. "Non-Hodgkin's lymphoma has a survival rate of . . . yyyyowsah . . ." (He does a double take.)

JONI: What? What does it say?

GARY: (To the librarian) So what are you doing for Thanksgiving? (Joni whacks herself over the head with the book and falls back unconscious. Cross-fade to stars, nebulae, eerie music.)

VOICE FROM BEYOND: Cancer. The final frontier. These are the voyages of the starship *Anesthetize*. Our five-year mission: To last another five years! To seek out new life— or hang on to the old one as long as we can, to boldly go where no scalpel has gone before!

(The starship warps past, flashing the title in its wake: "SCAR TREK!")

SOPRANO: ... *ah-AH-ah-ahahaha* ...

(Cut to oncologist's office, where Joni sits on a table wearing two paper napkins and a piece of string. The door zips open with a *zwheeesh*, and the oncologist enters wearing titanium lab coat and Vulcan ears.)

JONI: I have cancer.

ONCOLOGIST: Affirmative. (Scanning her with a tricorder.) Readings indicate an alien presence on both sides of the neck.

JONI: Am I going to die?

ONCOLOGIST: Biomedical scans confirm cellular assimilation is already extensive; however, it would be illogical to project an outcome without sufficient data. According to my calculations, an aggressive course of chemotherapy is indicated to maximize probability of survival, but there are certain negative side effects and a risk of mortality that accompany the treatment itself.

JONI: What does that mean?

ONCOLOGIST: You pays yer money, you takes yer chances.

JONI: What are my other options?

ONCOLOGIST: Well, there's cremation. Or there are some lovely plots overlooking the landfill on the edge of town.

JONI: Beam me up, Scotty.

(Cut to happy faces of Gary, Joni, and kids in boxes. Music up and they sing chipperly.)

Here's the story . . . of a lovely lady
Whose lymphatic system got a nasty growth
when her cells mutated forming tumors
that wrapped around her throat . . .

(Cut to Joni at the elementary school PTO meeting.)

JONI: I have cancer.

MRS. BRADY: Lymphoma! That's the same thing Jackie O. died of! *Oo-la-la*, you little show-off!

ALICE: Just remember, dear, you've got to keep up a positive attitude! That which does not kill us makes us stronger!

MRS. BRADY: Mark that down on the PTO volunteer schedule, Alice. Joni Rodgers will be either stronger or dead.

ALICE: We'll just pencil her in for the spring bake sale. Say, do you know Sam the butcher?

JONI: I think he did my lymph node dissection.

ALICE: Well, Sam's neighbor's cousin's hairdresser's sister had that lymphoma thing, too.

JONI: Oh? How is she doing?

ALICE: She died. But she had a great attitude about it!

(Mrs. Brady begins to sing a heartfelt rendition of "His Eye Is on the Sparrow.")

ALICE: Coffee anyone?

JONI: I'll have a mocha morphine, please.

MRS. BRADY: Now with Jackie, was that an oblivious-to-all-dignity-drugged-out-of-her-mind death or a horrifically-cognizant-of-every-unthinkably-agonizing-moment death?

ALICE: I heard it was agonizing. Excruciating, in fact.

JONI: Boy, that's a lovely pageboy you're wearing, Carol.

Where did you say you got that done?

MRS. BRADY: She must have felt like she'd descended into the bowels of hell.

ALICE: But what a trooper!

JONI: So what's on the ol' agenda here today? Any new business? New business anyone?

ALICE: Even as the cancer literally consumed her entire body. Like a rat gnawing at a loaf of bread. Gnawing and nibbling, day and night. . . .

(Music. Scenes of Joni smiling as she rolls up her sleeve for the phlebotomist, then standing in the chest X ray, drinking a large canister of barium.)

Who can turn the world on with her smile?

Who can take an X-ray plate and suddenly make it more like "X-file"?

It's malignant and you should know it

Each biopsy and every little CAT scan will show it

Cancer cells abound, though doctors missed 'em

Permeating your lymphatic system.

Ain't gonna make it after all. . . .

(Crossing the street in front of the hospital, Joni tosses her cap in the air, and her hair goes with it. Cut to Joni talking on the phone with Mom and Dad.)

JONI: I have cancer.

MOM: *Waaaaaaaaaaaaaaaaaaaahhhhhhhhhhhh!*

JONI: *Bloooyer melzen* disease *obner* non-Hodgkin's lymphoma. *Slim cooby mingo* lymphatic system.

MOM: *Waaaaaaaaaaaaaaaaaaaahhhhhhhhhhhh!*

JONI: It's okay, Mom. His eye is on the stronger! That which does not kill us makes us sparrow! I ain't down yet. I'm unsinkable! I dream the impossible dream! I'll never

walk alone! (She bursts into song.) "Tooooooo-morrow!
Too-morrow! I love ya, too-morrow!"

DAD: That's my girl. What a terrific attitude!

(Cut to Joni on the phone with sister.)

JONI: I have cancer.

JANIS: Okay. All right. So now at least you know what
you're up against. That's a good thing.

JONI: Yeah. I guess.

JANIS: Whatever's on your plate, Joni, I know you can handle it. How are you feeling so far?

JONI: Physically okay. And I'm not really upset. I just feel
sort of . . . disconnected. It's like—well, sometimes when
I'm in a play, I'll have this nightmare where I step out onstage, and the show is in progress. Only it's not the show I
thought I was in, so I don't know who I'm supposed to be
playing, and I have to try to fake it and come up with the
lines I think I'm supposed to say and make people laugh
and pretend I know what I'm doing so nobody will know
I'm really . . . dying.

JANIS: You're not dying.

JONI: I don't know. I'm not sure I can survive this.

JANIS: Yes, you can. You can do this," she said. "This you
can do."

My sister has a voice somewhere between Lauren Bacall
and the color mahogany. It fuses her woman's heart with a
precise executive diction that always sounds like she knows
what she's talking about. With that voice at my ear, I've
scribbled down recipes, directions, and book references. I
quote her to my children and imitate her delivery when nego-
tiating with used car salesmen, school principals, and other
fractious adults.

Now I closed my eyes and listened, pretending we were

lying side by side in the pastel-colored bedroom we used to share, our twin beds separated by a small alley the width of a woven pink-and-green rug. Even then, nightmares were the downside of my vivid imagination, and when I woke up screaming, she talked that voice across the darkness to me, telling me it was all right, and then it was.

When we were older, we'd lie in bed with the twilight window open above us, and she would try to tell me about coordinating the right clothes and not slouching, lest one make oneself look even more flat-chested, and that maybe a boy would ask me out if I wasn't so belligerent about my politics. She was my big sister. She dutifully took it as her lot in life to make a path that I could follow to find myself. I was her little sister. I took it as my lot in life to provide a dowdy backdrop against which she could showcase her physical, academic, and moral superiority. She called me on my misconceptions, pointed out my fashion faux pas. When we were teenagers, I hated how there was no hiding from her, how she always knew exactly where I was, especially when I was somewhere I ought not to be.

But when I was small, when we were playing the Witch and the Children beneath the clothesline, and the sheets billowed between us, and the witch was on the way—then it was good to know that she would always find me. That she would come. Just when the brightness of the sun became more piercing than warm, and the blue-clean walls closed in to keep me away from everyone in the world, when the phantom shirtsleeves reached and clawed, and still I crouched there, silent screaming, my mouth and heart both frozen open—just then, she would lift the white curtain, and there would be me, and I would remember that it was only a game.

Sitting on the floor with the phone tucked into my shoulder, arms wrapped around my knees, I felt that same way now. Tired. Small. Needing to be found. I rested my head against the blue-clean wall.

"If there's anything I can do to help—" she started, but immediately recognized how empty that phrase is. Of course, there's always something you can do to help, but the person who needs it is most likely not going to start making a laundry list of suggestions. Janis efficiently homed in on something specific to offer. "I'm going to hire someone to clean your house."

"No, don't do that. It's too expensive."

"That's what I'm going to do," she decreed over the top of my polite refusal. "You need to channel your energy into more important things. If I was there, I would do it myself, but I'm not there. Do you need me to come there?"

"No. No, everybody should just keep on with their life. Hopefully, it won't be too bad. And it's only six months. A person can stand just about anything for six months, don't you think?"

"Sure. Of course. But nonetheless—I'm sending someone to clean."

I nodded, knowing she could hear me without my saying a word.

Janis asked me again what the oncologist said, what the otolaryngologist said, what the radiologist said, helping me decipher the statistics and acronyms.

"It's too bad Berlitz doesn't have a course for this," I commented. "Sprechen Sie *Cancer?*"

"There you go," Janis said dryly.

"A set of audiotapes with a pocket-size English-Cancer/Cancer-English dictionary."

Interpreting the information with a film producer's bottom-line calm, Janis recast the cold oncologist as "professional" and our panicked mother as "justifiably concerned."

It was as close as anyone came to telling me, "Everything's going to be all right." And I desperately needed someone to tell me that. It would have been nice coming from an oncologist, but at this point, I was ready to settle for anyone short of Kevorkian.

"Well, I should go," I said after a while. "I've got to make an important phone call to the Psychic Friends Network."

Janis laughed. We talked for a few minutes more, and then I finally let her go. I hung up the phone and went into the bathroom.

"I have cancer," I told the mirror, and the mirror didn't move.

"Everything's going to be all right," I told myself, but my self had lost all credibility.

4

Hairless in Houston

And while she feels the heavens lie bare,
She only talks about her hair.

—FRANCIS THOMPSON

*T*exas is big. Dang big.

Why, there ain't nuthin' from Mary Kay to New York City bigger than what we got down here. We got big meat, big bugs, big cars, and big, big hair.

Why, Houston women have hair so big . . .

"How big is it?"

It's so big, it gives the Houston honeybees beehive envy. Some women have to get breast implants to maintain their balance. That's why Houston women have such tiny feet; things just don't grow that well in the shade. A true Texan woman cruises down the aisle at Mervyn's like the Snoopy balloon in the Macy's Thanksgiving Day parade; that bouffant would lift her right off the ground if her six children didn't have her tethered by the hand.

It takes a big-haired woman to satisfy a big-truckin'

man. You can't become a communicate member of the Baptist Church without it. It's essential to any waitressing job, prerequisite for a real estate license. It's as natural as Naugahyde, as artistically important as Elvis; a proud symbol of our feminine bounty and Christian largess. And it's not just the women. A meeting of the Houston Rotary Club could easily be mistaken for a national convention of TV evangelists. Big hair is the last magnolia-scented echo of our antebellum hoop-skirt opulence, and we'd rather add another area code to the local phone book than give it up.

Needless to say, it's not much fun being a bald girl in the Big Hair Capital of America.

*M*y oncologist's nurse was an enormous, easy-laughing woman named Yolanda. At first I thought it might be a little insensitive of her to wear her high, ultrasculpted, Afri-chic hairdos around all these bald people, but I later looked forward to seeing what her cranial topiary would do next. It held an almost hypnotic power; the mystery of Stonehenge, the magnificence of Lady Liberty. Solidified by some kind of industrial-strength lacquer, it confabulated in waves, curls, and wings, sometimes cascading from crown to nape with the attitude of a waterfall, sometimes towering above her fabulous face like an offshore oil rig.

I liked Yolanda. I think the gravity of her patients' situations lifted her out of the typical officio-clerical torpor and caused her to connect with them as human beings, which probably wasn't always good for her. It probably helped, however, that her patients were all in the process of developing unusually high pain thresholds. No yelping over one little needle stick or another; we had bigger fish to fry. Since all who enter there are loyal customers for the rest of their lives (however short or long the duration), she came to know names. "How are you feeling?" she'd always ask and "How are the kids?" Her care extended to the shell-shocked chauffeurs and loved ones who accompanied us. Yolanda and Gary quickly developed a wise-cracking camaraderie, exchanging barbs and pleasantries until the doctor came in.

It was hard to tell who was in charge most of the time; tall, broad-beamed Yolanda or the tiny oncologist, Dr. Jungsil Ro, who wore the feminine brown bob of a hummingbird and was as reserved and pastel as a bamboo painting. Her exotic accent made each word sound like something delicious to eat: a symptom from column A, a side effect from column B. Small and soft-spoken with dark almond-shaped eyes, Dr. Ro projected intelligence, professionalism, and very little else. Her concern reflected dedication without a hint of pity. Her questions and answers dealt with that part of me which was affected by cancer and nothing else.

"Brrr," Gary said when she went out of the room during our first visit.

"If I want someone to cry over me, I have my mother on the phone every night," I said. "Personally, I find Dr. Ro's lack of panic very reassuring."

"We show that much compassion for the airplanes down at the hangar," Gary commented.

"Well, I hope you're also as thorough."

"You doing okay?" He squeezed my shoulder.

"Yeah."

"Wanna make a break for it? Seriously. I think I can take Yolanda."

It was tempting, but I got dressed, and we went to a little conference room where Dr. Ro made a concise explanation of the diagnosis: diffuse large-cell lymphoma, a high-grade, swiftly spreading cancer of the lymphatic system. CAT scans revealed the cancer had metastasized from the original site to both sides of my neck, spreading downward toward my chest. Had it reached the diaphragm, my prognosis would have been much less hopeful, she explained, but I was having trouble taking a lot of comfort in that.

"So what does this mean?" I asked. "Does this mean . . . am I dying?"

But Dr. Ro was reluctant to place a statistical probability on my survival, dodging the question with cautionary statements like, "This is a very serious situation" and "It is important that we move ahead quickly." Chemotherapy, she said, had proved successful in such cases, and she was ordering six to eight cycles, for starters, to be followed, if needed, by additional cycles, finishing with radiation as sort of an isotopic cherry on top.

"No," I told her. "I don't want chemotherapy. I want to investigate my alternatives."

"Your alternatives," she put it bluntly, "are chemotherapy or death."

"Well, what about—I mean . . . alternative . . . *alternatives*," I stammered, taken aback. "Like herbal stuff and—and . . . stuff."

"Please," she interrupted, "you must not waste time on any such quackery as that. You are diagnosed early. You have very good chance of getting remission with chemotherapy. These other methods have no evidence of working. Only anecdotal evidence."

"But I read in this book—it said chemotherapy is like removing a wart with a blowtorch."

"That's not an appropriate comparison. A wart doesn't kill you."

"They said that nutrition and meditation—"

"Nutrition is very important. Meditation, yes. Because to relax is also very important. Not to be depressed, not to be afraid. But all this is *with* chemotherapy, not instead of. I have seen many people waste this time and then come back for chemotherapy when it is too late. Then it is much more difficult to achieve remission." Her eyes never wavered from mine, and they held not a trace of apology, sympathy, or doubt. "Perhaps you should read in medical journals," she said. "Scientific information on success of chemotherapy in lymphoma. Very good success."

I had read them. Their definition of success was five years. My definition had more to do with visiting Europe, seeing my grandchildren, and collecting Social Security. I looked to Gary, but there was no help there. On the way down, he'd already expressed his preference that I do whatever the oncologist told me.

"I know most people won't make the changes. Or they start out, and then they don't stick to it." I started begging like a child in the grocery store. Closing in on the candy aisle. Knowing what Mom is going to say and not liking it. "But I would. I'd meditate every day and become a vegetarian and—"

"How will you do this if you are dead?"

"That's the only way I'd become a vegetarian," Gary contributed.

"But the chemo is—it's so . . ." Adequate adjectives eluded me.

"It is an aggressive procedure," Dr. Ro conceded. "This is an aggressive disease."

"What sort of side effects are we talking about?" Gary asked.

I tried to listen, but didn't feel like I was absorbing much as she laid out the gruesome possibilities in clinical nomenclature, couching blunt realities like "barfing" and "agony" in palatable terms like "nausea" and "discomfort." This was the first time I heard the word *alopecia*. It sounded like something you'd find growing in an English country garden.

The alopecia are in bloom a-gain. Such a delicate flow-ah.

Or like a character in a Jane Austen novel.

Miss Alopecia Pinsford has invited us to tea at Vincristine Manor.

As soon as I heard the word, it started going through my head to the tune of that little French folk song, *"Allouette."*

Alopecia, gentille alopecia . . . Alopecia, je te plumeria!

"What's alopecia?" Gary asked.

"The loss of one's hair," Dr. Ro said without hesitation or sentiment.

"Oh yeah. That," Gary said. "So she'll be completely . . ."

He stopped short of the word that starts with *B* and rhymes with "appalled." That thing that makes grown men cry and keeps Sy Sperling in Armani.

"Not everyone loses all hair with chemo," said Dr. Ro. "Studies show that a certain percentage of people are not affected."

"Have you ever treated anyone who wasn't?" I inquired skeptically.

"No," she had to admit. "But studies show a certain percentage."

"It doesn't matter," I said stiffly. "That's the least of my worries."

"When can she start?" Gary asked. "Can she start tomorrow?"

Dr. Ro described the CHOP+Bleo regimen, told us what the letters stood for, explained how each cycle would work. I was to return the next day.

"Day one" she called it.

Today is the first day of the end of your life, I grimly paraphrased to myself.

After bone marrow was surgically extracted for biopsy, a longline would be inserted in my arm; a cath port permanently sutured to my forearm would access this tiny tube that extended inside the vein, traveling up and over into my chest. Through it, I would receive the Radioactive Cocktail. Several daily doses of the steroid Prednisone were to be taken on days 1 through 5, and on day 5, an intravenous "Bleo Booster" would round out the kamikaze logic of each chemo cycle. Days 6 through 21 would be spent watching my white count plummet like a bear market and then, bolstered as needed by bone marrow stimulants, bull its way back enough to start the process over again.

Plainly and in detail, she outlined the agenda for the destruction of the world as I knew it. She didn't seem to be in a state of panic. She didn't appear to feel sorry for me. She didn't seem to notice I was in the process of being smote by God, a pathetic little dinghy on the storm-tossed ocean of ill fate.

"I guess this is all in a day's work for you," I snipped.

"Yes," she nodded with a small smile, thinking perhaps that I'd meant to compliment her or maybe even that I would find it reassuring to know I was just another Chiclet in the great masticating maw of industrial medicine.

"These may be of some help," she said, handing me a stack of booklets and pamphlets. The first one, the publication of which had been generously underwritten by (who else?) a pharmaceutical company, was delicately titled *Chemotherapy and Me.* I stared at the medicine-colored cover. Chemotherapy and me? Chemotherapy and *ME?*

No.

No, it should be *Chemotherapy and Somebody Else. Chemotherapy and People Who Deserve It.*

Chemotherapy and Telephone Solicitors.

Chemotherapy and People Who Talk During Movies.

Chemotherapy and Girls Who Made Fun of Me in High School.

Not chemotherapy and *me*!

Beneath it was a second booklet, alarmingly titled *Coping with Chronic Pain*. I hastily shuffled that aside only to unearth *Coping with End of Life Issues*.

"Side effects are usually minimal the first cycle or two, so it is wise to eat well then," Dr. Ro advised. She left the rest unsaid.

*T*he next day, I lay in the surgical suite, Puccini's *Madama Butterfly* in my Walkman headphones extolling the heroine's dream of *un bel di* when the long-awaited lover she thought had taken her for his wife would return in a tall ship.

Yeah, don't bet on it, sweet cakes, I sulked, tasting a bitter kinship with the doomed soprano as I awaited the return of Dr. Ro, who was off preparing the hardware she was going to use to extract a marrow sample from my hipbone. *He's already married to some WASP from the Hamptons, and I'm about to—*

"What's that?" I asked a nurse who was pushing a syringe of something into my IV.

"Just a little Demerol to help—"

"Oh no! I'm allergic to Demerol!"

"*What*? Are you sure?"

"Well, yes, I'm *sure*! Look—it's on my chart. I made sure they put it on there."

She seized my chart from a nearby table, bit back an expletive, and rushed out of the room. I heard Yolanda's

47

raised voice in the hallway, then a calm undercurrent I knew was Dr. Ro. A few minutes later, they all came in, and Dr. Ro took my hand as Yolanda pushed another syringe into the IV.

"That was unfortunate," she said. "I apologize. This should curtail any reaction, but we'll wait a while before we begin the procedure. Just to know everything is fine."

I nodded, wide-eyed, my confidence in the well-oiled machine slightly shaken. As the megadose of antihistamine drew shades down over my eyes, I drifted back into the arms of Madama Butterfly. Criminy. What was she catterwalling about now?

All that unrelenting hope was heartbreaking, the mood I was in now, but the soaring music slowly lifted my consciousness just north of the stitches in my throat, and later, it helped drown out the sound of the electric drill Dr. Ro was using to mine for the marrow sample.

"You must remain still now," she said, gently lifting one side of the headphones, and I nodded.

I thought about making some smart remark about how I would really be holier than thou after this, but it seemed like a better idea to focus on the pattern of my breathing. As Madam B. plunged the knife into her own heart, Dr. Ro inserted a long needle into the mine shaft and aspirated the sample.

"It's finished now," she said a few minutes later, stroking my arm with her gloved hand as the nurse closed the incision and applied dressing to my hip. "You tolerated the procedure very well."

"I have a very high threshold," I lied to everyone in the room, including myself.

"It's unfortunate these allergies you have. Demerol, Darvon, Codeine. If you could take them, these are good for pain."

"So is Puccini," I shrugged. "And he doesn't give me hives."

"What opera is this?"

"Oh, it's my favorite. *Madame Butterfly*."

"Ah," she nodded, but without enthusiasm.

"You don't like opera?"

"Oh yes," she said. "But this opera . . . this opera and the modern version—"

"*Miss Saigon*."

"Yes. My son took me to see *Miss Saigon*. I dislike this portrayal of the Asian woman."

"But she's so beautiful and noble . . ."

"To kill herself? This is not very noble to me, sacrificing herself for a man who throws her away. I don't know any women like this. I know women who fight." As she spoke, she set aside the bloodied instruments and removed her latex gloves. Her hands were cool then, soft with the powder from the inside of the latex, but strong as she took my arm and helped me sit up on the edge of the table.

"I think you are a woman who fights," she said.

If she'd stood there one moment longer, all *human being* like that, I'd have thrown my arms around her and started sobbing.

My next stop was the lab, where I received my longline. I plugged Count Basie into the Walkman for that one, but toward the end, they made me take it off, stood me in front of the X-ray machine, and inserted a thin metal wire through the line to make sure it was going where it was supposed to go. When the technician shucked the film onto the lighted screen, there it was, sure enough: a little subway line leading from a downtown stop in my forearm to the Grand Central Station of my heart.

At the chemo clinic, a nurse led me to a recliner and hung an IV bag on the tree next to it. Her name was Helena, she said, and I decided to take that as a good omen.

"It's so nice to have that longline, isn't it?" She smiled, and in response to my incredulous gaze, she added, "You wouldn't want to get stuck every time, would you?"

"You're right," I said, remembering Sid's tales of being stuck in her wrists, hands, feet, and neck when the veins in her arms finally gave out. "I guess it is nice. It just took me a minute to shift into a paradigm where I could appreciate something like that."

"This is just saline solution." She indicated the bag hanging like Eve's first fruit on the IV tree. "And this," she whipped out a syringe, "is a little something for nausea. It'll help you relax."

Holding the syringe in one hand and my cath port in the other, she had to remove the cap from the needle with her teeth, which gave me the willies worse than the sight of her jabbing it into the longline port.

"We'll give that a minute to kick in while I go get the rest."

With Jimi Hendrix howling in my headphones, I was beginning to see auras around Gary and around the other patients in their recliners by the time she returned to replace the saline with an amber bag of . . . something scary. Eye of Newt. Over the next several hours, she came and went, checking the flow, taking my blood pressure, telling me what was in each bag as she hoisted it onto the tree.

"Here's the Vincristine."

"Wow," I quipped blearily, "I could have had a V-8."

"Here's the Cytoxin," she announced a while later. (Note to future pharmaceutical marketing staff: there is something distinctly off-putting about the suffix -*toxin*. I'm certain focus groups would bear me out on this.)

"Hey," I mumbled, "I thought I ordered a Bud Lite."

A strange metallic-tasting cloud had begun to gather at the back of my nose and throat, and an odd gray sensation seeped out toward my extremities, as if I were being slowly turned to stone. I tried to perceive the feeling as heat, tried to visualize a backfire being set to burn off a safe zone between myself and the rampant wildfire.

I drifted off, coming around in time to hear her tell Gary, "Here's the first dose of Bleomycin. She'll be back for a Bleo booster in five days."

I closed my eyes again. *With a name like Bleo, it's gotta be good* . . . .

Before I left, she connected a portable computerized pump to the cath port. It would hang from a blue nylon shoulder strap, dispensing tiny doses of Adriamycin over the next forty-eight hours.

"This is the stuff that makes your hair fall out," she said.

"Oh?" I couldn't wait to hear the positive spin she was going to put on that one.

Instead she quoted from the book of Matthew. "But even the very hairs of your head are numbered. So do not be afraid, for you are worth more than many sparrows."

"Hey, no more painful bikini wax," I woozed. "Lemony fresh Adria removes unsightly hair and leaves you silky smooth *aaaalllllll* over."

It felt like a ritual of blessing, the way she held my arm, then hung the shoulder strap around my neck as if she were decorating me with a medallion.

"Now, this pump has to be carefully maintained," another nurse explained to Gary, recognizing I was still a little psychedelic. "Adria is roughly the same stuff as mustard gas. It mustn't be allowed to leak or touch anything."

Except, of course, me and my mutant innards.

"The home health nurse will be by day after tomorrow to take it off her and change the dressing on the sutures and answer any questions you might have." She took my hand and called out loudly, as if I were deaf or catatonic or had Alzhiemer's or something. "THIS IS YOUR PUMP, JONI. ISN'T IT GREAT?"

"OH YEAH. SUPER."

"You can only take the Adria a little at a time," Helena said, gently shifting my paradigm yet again. "You wouldn't want to sit in the hospital for three days, would you?"

On the way home, I flipped the tape over to start *Madama Butterfly* again, but found I couldn't listen to all that heartbreaking hope without hearing the echo of a hand-held drill in the background.

*T*he first thing to go was my pubic hair. This caught me by surprise. For some reason, it hadn't occurred to me that "one's hair" meant *down there* hair.

Even more surprising was Gary's reaction. The ol' kinkster actually found my denuded pudendum quite enticing, and happily, I was still feeling well enough to make the most of his newfound fetish. Unhappily, this delectable defoliation also confirmed that I was not destined to be counted among the "certain percentage."

I spent a lot of time at the mirror during the next few days, brushing, French braiding, unbraiding, stoling my long hair forward over my shoulders like a mink, pulling it straight back from my face, trying to envision what I would look like. Sinead O'Connor? Caroll O'Connor? A casaba melon with contact lenses?

This is really stupid, I reprimanded myself. *It's just hair. It grows back.*

A day or two before my second treatment, I asked my downstairs neighbor, a beautiful beautician named Vida, to bind my auburn tresses into eleven long braids and cut them off half an inch from my scalp. It seemed like the logical thing to do. The approach that says, "You can't fire me, I quit!"

"Are you sure about this?" Vida paused the scissors just above my head and posed the impossible question.

"I'm sure," I said. "Sure. I'm sure. 'Cause I really think this will ease the transition for my kids, you know? And believe me, losing my hair is the least of my worries. And it'll be so much easier to take care of this way. This thing in my arm has to stay dry, so it's impossible to shampoo or anything. And when the stubble falls out, who cares? I'll be losing short, stubbly, ugly hair, not some beautiful crowning glory, so . . . who cares. It's just hair. It's just vanity. It grows back. It's just hair. Everything's going to be all right."

When Vida was gone, I laid the braids on wax paper and wrapped them with robotic precision in a long, straight bundle, folding factory-neat creases, smoothing symmetrical edges. I sat for a while with the package in my lap, then laid it in a desk drawer and slid the drawer shut.

*T*en days later, when I stroked my hand across my crown, stubble trinkled into the sink like needles off last year's Christmas tree, and the adhesive lint roller I'd been using instead of a brush left broad, white tracks of bare scalp.

"Wow," Gary said. "It's like . . . Comanche aftermath."

My dear darling husband has his own special way of combining the sensitivity of a cue ball with the political correctness of a dwarf-tossing tournament. You gotta love him.

I stepped into the shower, gently rubbed with a wash-cloth for a minute or two, rinsed the cloth, rubbed a little more, rinsed. When I stepped out from behind the plastic curtain, I was as bald as Warbucks.

"Geez," Gary gulped. "Holy shit."

"Hey, honey! *Woop, woop, woop!*" I did the Three Stooges face-blabbering thing and laughed uncomfortably. Gary just stood there.

"It's okay," I assured him. "Really, it's fine."

"Holy shit," he repeated.

"Gee honey, you always know the right thing to say." I cleared a wad of reddish brown stubble from the drain and dropped it in the toilet. "Thanks a lot, ya big ham stack."

"Sorry," Gary mumbled.

"What's the matter? Did *alopecia* suddenly lose its erotic charm?" I asked harshly, knowing that if alopecia in particular had not, I in general most certainly had.

"I'm sorry. It's just—it's so . . . so *evident* now. There's no more denying how sick you are."

"I'm not *sick*. Don't say it like that."

"You're sick, Joni."

"*I'm not sick!*"

"What do you mean you're not sick? You have *cancer* for Christ's sake!"

"Oh, real nice. Throw *that* in my face, why don't you?"

"You're sick. And you're gonna get a lot sicker before this whole thing is over."

I started slamming drawers open and closed, searching for something I could wear that would make me look like someone who still had blood in her veins.

"I'm not *sick,* and I don't need you looking at me think-ing *Aagh! Yuck! She's sick! She's sick! Oh my God, she's dying!*"

"I don't think that!"

"Don't you?"

"No! If I thought that, I couldn't . . . I would . . ." He drew a towel from the cupboard and wrapped it around me. "I don't think that."

"I don't need your patronizing tone of voice, either."

"I'm sorry." He took another towel and knelt down to dry my dripping legs.

"And I don't need you to take me out of the bathtub like I'm one of the kids. Would you just—*stop that!*"

We tug-o'-warred with the towel, but his hands were stronger than mine.

"Stand still," he barked. "I'm being supportive. I'm a supportive, sensitive kind of guy."

"You are not. A sensitive kind of guy would be hugging me right now."

"Yes, O Shiny-Pated One," he said, and pulled me into his arms; the only thing I could wear that made me feel like someone who still had blood in her veins.

We decided to go to the health club and work out, as planned. I rummaged in the box of scarves sent by a host of well-wishers and selected one sent to me by my sister, Linda, along with some of her homegrown herbal remedies. The soft fabric was vibrant blue with psychedelic fish. I tied it over my head and looked in the mirror. I looked like the cover of a Who album. I could hear hallucinogenic guitar solos on tracks like "Brain Swim" and "Fisher of Rolando."

A large square of sepia silk patterned with delicate cherry blossoms and feathering twigs made me look like someone who *knows all, tells all.*

"Gaze into my crystal ball," I told the mirror. "Or just use my head."

A long, pale mist of chiffon lent a pre-*Sunset Boulevard* Carol-Burnett-as-Gloria-Swanson look.

"Max, I'm ready for my close-up."

A bright green beret made me look like a gay GI Joe.

I was Forrest Gump in a blue baseball cap. An' that's all ah have t'say about that.

The primitive pattern headwrap took me the way of the Ubangi. *Bwana! Bwana!*

"Yes, I Bwana. I bwana have my hair back."

I closed the box and studied my reflection. Joni Rodgers: Unplugged.

Or was it? No . . . no, that wasn't me standing there. It was . . . it was *Emil Lonnquist!* My paternal grandfather, fresh off the boat from Sweden. Here he was. Right here in my bathroom mirror. A dashing young Emil who lived long before the old man came with his faltering hands, offering all the grandkids candy from a McCoy cookie jar. I recognized him from the sepia-tone photos framed on the sideboard and walls of grandma's house in Minneapolis. Those were indisputably Emil's ears bracketing his high cheekbones, and those were his temples and forehead. But the ears lay back nicely against the head, and the head had a pretty good shape overall. And I'd never noticed before now how large and green his eyes were.

"*Ya, g'dagen, poikan,*" I nodded, imitating the lilting accent that always used to remind me of a musical saw. I brushed my teeth and put on a little makeup. Not too bad.

See? I congratulated myself; no big deal. I've only been bald forty-five minutes, and I'm already used to it.

But knowing it might take the rest of the world a little longer to adjust, I took out a red bandana and fashioned it into the punk yarmulke Demi Moore would one day make fabulous.

On me it just looked like Harley Dude.

"Born to be wi-i-i-i-ild. . . ."

*H*alfway through my twenty minutes on the treadmill, I took off the bandana. Trudging on that torture rack was getting tougher by the day as it was, and a double sheath of stifling fabric instead of the micro-short hair I'd gotten used to—it was just too dang hot.

What is this, Iran? I reasoned, avoiding the eyes of everyone around me. *I have to cover my head to keep from offending my betters?*

Silently rehearsing clever retorts to imaginary affronts, I finished my walk and went to the weights. (The puny parcels I was lifting actually stretch the definition of the word *weight*, but attendance ought to count for something.) I noticed a woman staring at me from a stationary bike. I focused on breathing in on the release, exhaling with the lift. Sweat chilled on top of my head as the air-conditioner kicked on.

The locker room reverberated with laughter and conversation. Ladies all around me were brushing and blow-drying, teasing and spritzing, as I stepped out of the shower and peeled the plastic bag from my arm, carefully dabbing drips away from the cath port.

"He's the only one who ever cuts my bangs right," one woman was raving about a beautician named Caesario. "I don't let anyone cut my hair who isn't flamingly gay. You know how artistic they always are."

This was the enthusiastic consensus all around, but when I came to the mirror, everyone abruptly stopped talking. Pained silence rolled in like a fog bank.

"Whatever you do," I said ominously, "don't piss him off." I settled a straw Panama on my naked head and added, "You know how emotional they always are."

She nodded slightly, and they all dragged their eyes away from my head, mental wheels spinning, until someone behind us started laughing. It was the stationary bike woman. I went around a bank of lockers and sat down to tie my shoes. She came over and started stuffing sweaty spandex into her worn duffel.

"How long have you been in chemo?" she asked.

"Is it that obvious? There goes my lawsuit against Vidal Sassoon."

She laughed again and sat down beside me.

"It's not obvious. But I had breast cancer four years ago. It's all pretty familiar to me. By the way," she added, "I'm Karen." It comforted me to know her name was still Karen, even after she had cancer.

"I'm Joni."

I hadn't yet discovered that cancer is the best little conversation starter since "What's your sign?" so the instant camaraderie was unexpected. As we talked, I pulled up my sleeve to show her my cath port, she pulled down her collar to show me her scar. We compared chemo regimens and white counts, eventually moving out to the café area to negate our workouts with a couple of cappuccinos.

"You're brave to go without a hat like that," she commented.

"Not really. It was just too hot."

"Most women would take off their shirt in public before they'd go bald."

"Well, my head has a much better shape than my breasts do."

"I never had the nerve to go without my wig. No matter how hot and scratchy it got, I wore that thing till I had my old self back. I had a couple really nice ones. Betty Rubenstein."

"I'm afraid my budget is more like Betty Rubble. I'd probably get better results with a box of SOS pads and a staple gun."

"Did you know you can get them on loan at M.D. Anderson?"

"Yeah, but I have a deep abiding fear of wigs," I finally confessed. "I was in a play several years ago—*Ah, Wilderness!* by Eugene O'Neill. I played the old maid, Lily, who gets to dance with the lovable drunkard Sid, and one night, he spun me around, and my pompadour flew clear out to the front row like a great brown fruit bat."

Karen laughed so hard she aspirated a gulp of cappuccino and started coughing.

"It landed on somebody's lap and got tangled in her beaded evening bag," I recalled. "I just stood there thinking, 'This is not happening. This is a nightmare.'"

"Kind of like when they told you it was cancer?"

"Yeah," I sighed, "pretty much like that. Anyhow, I don't do wigs."

"You're brave," she said again. "You're like Cass Meyer."

"Who?"

"Cass Meyer. The newscaster on channel fifty-one. She went on TV and did a report about her chemo—no wig. Totally bald right there on TV. And she said, 'I have cancer, and the worst thing about it was losing my hair.' It was cool."

"That is cool," I agreed. "But 'the worst thing'? It's just hair. It's just vanity."

"No," she said. "It's not about vanity. It's about holding

on to anything *normal*. You might find . . . later on when it gets . . . later. You might need to hold on to small things. They matter. Because cancer can be very isolating. And those small things—they make you part of the same life everyone else is part of."

We sipped our coffee in silence for a bit, and I thought about my braids at home in a drawer.

"So," she smiled, "how does your husband feel about you going public with your new look?"

"Oh, unfortunately, he's not handling it very—" I stopped mid-sentence.

Gary's timing had apparently improved since earlier that day. He'd chosen this moment to come striding in the door of the café, grinning from sea to shining sea, his head freshly shaven.

"Hey baby," he said, bald as Warbucks. "*Woop, woop, woop!*"

*L*ater came, and I understood.

"I still have my eyebrows," I told my friend Lagenia, who'd survived Hodgkin's back when Hodgkin's was considered unsurvivable. "As long as I have my eyebrows, I'm okay. I'll just keep dangling from these eyebrows as they continue their normal life."

A few days later, my eyebrows fell out. I looked in the mirror and found an alien invader looking back at me. Yoda with a blue dress on. *Klatu barata nikto.*

"E.T. phone home," I made the mistake of saying, and it made the kids giggle so deliciously, I gave in when they kept urging me to "Do it again, Mommy, do it again!"

"*Bless us and splash us, my precious!*" Gary slavered an impression of Tolkien's slick-headed Gollum.

I rarely went anywhere without my turban then. I rarely went anywhere *with* my turban, for that matter. Without sheltering lashes, my eyes were constantly irritated by dust and debris, and the desolation of my barren face in the mirror was too painful to look at. I wore this void like mourning black, and most people responded to it with the same deference. A dropping away of the eyes, a sympathetic quiet. The isolation Karen spoke of was born out of my own grief and anger as much as the sympathy and fear of others, but I was lonely.

Painfully lonely.

Eleanor Rigby lonely.

Maytag repairman lonely.

Having just moved to Houston a couple months before my diagnosis, I really hadn't had time to forge much of a support network there, and it was a little tricky striking up new acquaintances in my condition.

"Hi, I'm Joni, and I'm a sucking black hole of emotional need right now. My hobbies are taking drugs, napping, and calling people I hardly know for emergency child-care. Wanna be my friend?"

It was tempting to hang a wreath on the door and stay inside for a while. At least until my eyebrows grew back.

When one of the townsfolk died in Victorian times, it was customary for neighbors to spread straw in the cobblestone street outside their home to muffle the sounds of the horses and carriages and clattering wagons that passed by. It was a loving gesture, a sign of respect, but oh, how lonely it must have been to sit in that silent house where the wreath on the door announced *death is here* and the muted bell welcomed only the whispering mourners.

I opened the drawer in which I'd secreted my braids and

unrolled them from the wax paper sheath, seeing what I hadn't seen all the mornings and nights I'd brushed and plaited this hair, all the moments I'd felt Gary's fingers tangled through it, his mouth moving against it. It wasn't exceptionally beautiful hair; a benign auburn brown with more than a few strands of gray. I'd colored it too often and cussed it daily. Many was the time I delivered it into the hands of whatever ten-dollar yahoo was working at the strip mall hair whacker—or worse yet, wielded the scissors myself, invariably pruning the bangs way too short while in the hissy throws of hormone-induced dementia. I used to hate my hair because it was so ordinary, and I hadn't yet learned the value of ordinary things. I was so busy striving to be exceptional, I missed the dance of the everyday, the red-brown grace of the gloriously mundane.

"It'll grow back," I kept reassuring myself. "It'll all grow back."

*H*ome-cooked dinners—at least those cooked by me—were few and far between as the undertow of treatment-related fatigue began to drag me down, but I made my best effort one evening to produce a respectable Southwestern chicken chili. I'd purchased some dried ancho peppers at Fiesta and crushed them between my palms over the Crock-Pot for the final touch. I rinsed a few dishes, then feeling light-headed, sat down at the table, resting with my head in my hands. I was just beginning to drift when the searing heat of the pepper oils began to scorch across my chemo-sensitized scalp from the front of my forehead to the nape of my neck. I bolted to the sink and stuck my head under the faucet, suddenly sympathizing with Michael Jackson after that terrible incident with the pyrotechnic Pepsi commercial.

"Youch," Gary commiserated an hour later as he poured a gallon of cold milk over my still feverish head. "But the chili was excellent."

On another occasion, five minutes outside without a hat left my cranium crimson as a woodpecker's.

"Geez, feel that," I grimaced, dotting aloe across my flaming pate. "You could fry an egg on there."

"Hmm. Dinner and entertainment," he teased. "Who needs Vegas?"

My daily "Please let it grow back" prayer was amended to "Please let it grow back *faster*."

*I*n keeping with our tradition of beneficence and big-nitude, we Texans had ourselves a big, big summer that year. It hit like a lava flow and lasted longer than a roadkill armadillo, hotter than hell's vestibule and humid as a dog's mouth. I had ditched the turban by mid-May. If people were staring, I didn't know, didn't want to know, and didn't care. Being bald was better than sweltering under some stifling lid, even though bag boys and gas station attendants constantly called me "sir."

Mercifully, the last to leave were the first to be reborn; within a month or two after my last treatment, a stubby fringe of lashes revived, and above them came a faint hedge of brows that would have had women of the fifties madly plucking, and eventually, a dandelion halo of peach fuzz hair emerged up top.

I returned to the health club with a full stock of one-liners for the spritz crowd at the mirror.

"For God's sake, stay away from those home perms."

"So that's the last time I go to the salon on Neo-Nazi Day."

But along about October, they started commenting on my little micro-do. How cool and comfy it must be. How—um, how *perky* it looked. Yeah, really *perky*. How brave I was to get it cut so short. I rushed to explain that I hadn't done it on purpose, not sure which is the lesser of the two evils, cancer or a poor sense of style. I stopped hating them for having their huge hair. I even forgave them for complaining about it.

It really is a shame. Tiny hair is so perfectly suited to the climate of southeast Texas, where there are days so hot you feel overdressed in earrings and a smile. I fantasized that my little non-coif might start a revolution, or at least a fashion trend, but all you have to do is click back and forth between *Walker, Texas Ranger* and an old *Dallas* rerun to see that some things never change, and Houston hair volume is one of them.

5
Passion Slave: Secret Life of a Lymphomaniac

On cold days
it is easy to be reasonable,
to button the mouth against
kisses,
dust the breasts
with talcum powder
& forget
the red pulp meat
of the heart.

—ERICA JONG

*T*he summer after eighth grade, I was sitting on the bleachers at the Monroe County Fairgrounds in Tomah, Wisconsin, waiting for the Up With People concert to start, securely ensconced in a happy childhood, Nutty Buddy in one hand, Ferris wheel tickets in the other, when Billy Cato sat down next to me, and my entire body lit up like the Empire State Building. In bed that night, I couldn't find anyplace Christian to keep my hands. I drifted between amorous imaginings of Billy and shame-filled thoughts of going blind, then falling down a flight of stairs and going to hell. Certain I was the most sinful, disgusting harlot God had grieved over since Salome shook her can for King Herod, I tore my heart out for love of Billy all through high school. The more fully he filled his football jersey, the more skin gangster my feelings for him became. I knew if he had any such improper feelings for me something terrible was bound to happen, so I had to be horribly rude and hateful to him in order to protect myself, and then I had to feel horribly guilty for hurting someone I loved. The struggle to keep a lid on this unacceptable part of myself continued for years. Until I met Jon.

"You're not as nice as you'd like people to think you are," he whispered to me once in the thick of things. "There's someone completely obscene inside of you, and someday, somebody's gonna let her out." And then—God damn him and bless him and curse and preserve him!—he up and did it. He taught me how to celebrate myself, and when I met Gary, the celebration escalated to the connubial Mardi Gras that evolves when two people commit years to the process of growing to know each other.

It never even occurred to me I might someday lose that.

What little I was able to read about chemo-related changes in sexuality mostly dealt with how the partner should be patient, should tolerate the sick person's repulsive appearance and be satisfied with cuddling or some such crap, because obviously, the person with cancer would never want to have sex, even if she could find someone deviant enough to desire her. Apparently, people with cancer, being canonized in preparation for their premature death and subsequent sainthood, are supposed to become suddenly asexual. With one foot in the grave, we're expected to dwell primarily in the spiritual realm, but when I thought I was dying, I wanted to get as much of the physical world as I possibly could prior to making my departure.

During the first few weeks of chemo, Gary and I clung to each other, each frantic to get our mouths and hands on every inch of the other's body. As the *Titanic* Ballroom Band played a death waltz outside our bedroom door, we struggled to make every orgasm what you'd want your last orgasm to be. Then the adrenaline rush of diagnosis began to wear off. The heart-pounding fear numbed down to a grinding daily acceptance. My steroid-bloated body, swollen face, and evaporating hairline began to tell the never-ending story of fatigue, frustration, and a deep underlying sadness.

Gary tended my cath port site, kneeling beside the bed to remove the dressing and swab the sutures, employing all the tenderness with which he used to kneel between my legs to remove my clothing and stroke my skin. He pushed syringes of heparin into my cath port and pierced my hip with Neupogen injections, an unbearably sad parody of all the years he'd entered and infused me with his living muscle and sweat and semen and breath.

There was no loss of desire on my part. I wanted to make love, wanted to believe there was some part of me that cancer could not obliterate. I needed the parts of me that were still alive to stay that way.

On a more practical note, insomnia is a common side-effect of chemo, and we all know the best cure for insomnia is a bit of human comfort. When that comfort is lacking, people get cranky. They start pacing. They start referring to the shower massage as "Trevor." For this very reason, it's important that a woman be sufficiently . . . self-sufficient. Like they always say, "If you want something done right, do it yourself!"

But because the veins in my left arm were blown during the diagnostic testing process, my longline had to be installed in my right arm, and me being right-handed—well, whenever my arm was curved to a certain posture for a certain length of time with certain musculoskeletal activity of my hand and wrist causing certain reactions in my respiratory and circulatory systems, a constriction of the line would occur, setting off the alarm on my Adria pump. So just as Lady Chatterly is about to dissolve into a thousand galaxies—

MEEEEEB! MEEEEEB! MEEEEEB!

Her Pekinese is suddenly passing a kidney stone.

Never mind going blind, now I had to worry about hearing impairment. The sound was like microphone feedback, noon at the factory, Ozzy Osbourne with a sinus infection. Cold water enough when I was home alone; even more disinclining when it brought either Gary or my mother running from the next room.

Ah me. I eventually gave up.

It wasn't the orgasm I needed anyway. It was Gary. Let's face it—you can diddle yourself to carpal tunnel syndrome and still miss the one basic ingredient of human comfort: another human.

I didn't expect Gary to desire me on the really hideous barfy days, but there were plenty of good days in the early months. Days when we took the kids to the movies or scrounged for bargains at the local antique stores. On those days I still felt somewhat like myself, and Gary would take my hand, not just because he thought I was too weak to walk. On those days, I struggled to understand why we couldn't set it all aside for just half an hour, just set it outside our bedroom door for a precious few minutes.

So this was one of those days.

After we tucked the kids in bed, I put on a long-sleeved silk shirt to obscure the snaking IV that connected the Adria pump to my arm. I bound my head with a long silk scarf and let it trail down in front of my shoulder, just the way he used to love my hair to fall forward when I sat astride his lap. I applied the dark red lipstick he loved to see left on all parts of his anatomy, and when he came in to flush my cath port with heparin for the night, I presented myself to him, all bordello eyes and suggestive remarks.

He stood looking at me the way a beef cow looks at a Burger King.

"Okay. I know," I said, wanting to spare him the agony of saying anything, but not willing to let him get away. "But we could turn out the lights. It'll be dark. You won't have to look at me."

"It's not the way you look," he told me, even though I didn't believe it the first five hundred times he said so. "That has nothing to do with it."

"Then what is it?"

"It's—well . . . germs . . . you'd get my germs, and—and . . . I don't want to hurt you."

"You won't hurt me, bear. We'll be careful. We'll go slow. And I'll risk the germs, I don't care. Can't you understand, it hurts me more to not have you?"

"I'm sorry," he said to the floor. "I can't. I just feel like . . . a ghoul."

"A ghoul? What do you mean 'ghoul'?" I asked, knowing exactly what he meant, but wanting him to suffer. When he didn't answer, I turned sarcastic. "Poor boy! Went to bed with Auntie Mame and woke up with Uncle Fester."

Gary didn't say anything.

"I am not an ah-nee-mal!" I did my Elephant Man imitation, pulling the scarf off my head and stoking a little more ammo into the guilt cannon. "I am a man!"

"That's not funny."

"No, it's not! We've gone from comedy to horror."

Silence. The passive-aggressive body slam. He knew I couldn't stand that.

"You are such a fucking hypocrite!" I raged. "Oh, no, it has *nothing* to do with my looks. You're above that, aren't you? It doesn't matter at all that you used to look at me and think *tattoo chick*, and now you look at me and think *Fangoria*."

"No," he flared, "I look at you and think—"

"What?"

"Nothing."

"You think *death*."

Apparently, he hadn't read in the playbook that he was supposed to deny that. He just stood there, looking at the saline and heparin syringes in his hand.

"You think death," I said from the most hollow part of my heart. "And nobody wants to touch that."

*H*e came running, of course, when he heard the alarm.

MEEEEEB! MEEEEEB! MEEEEEB!

"Are you okay?"

"Yes," I called, wrestling my nightshirt down and scrabbling to a fetal position before he turned on the light.

"I heard the alarm go off."

"I just had my arm funny. Go back to your television."

Gary sat down on the edge of the bed.

"Let me look."

"No."

"Yes," he pushed. "I just want to make sure the connection is okay. If that stuff is leaking, it'll eat right through your skin."

"Fine," I sighed and rolled onto my back.

He unbuttoned the silk nightshirt, eased my arm out of the sleeve, following with his hand, feeding through the pump on its tether of plastic tubing. The pump chirped and whirred, releasing another tiny blast of Adriamycin. The *sssshhhh-sha-ka-sahh* sound always made Malachi and Jerusha say, "You took another picture, Mom."

"Seems to be running okay," Gary said, checking the digital readout.

"Yeah."

"Looks like about twelve hours to go. You probably won't feel too bad until tomorrow night."

"I'll be fine."

"Yeah." He examined the juncture where the IV joined into my cath port. "I'm just gonna tape that again."

He went to the walk-in closet, where one wall was now devoted to medical supplies shelved in plastic shoe boxes and came back with the clear surgical tape. After gently removing the layer that had been bollixed by my one-armed grapple to get into the nightshirt, he carefully positioned the IV apparatus and strapped the juncture solidly onto my forearm.

"There," he said. "Feel a little more secure now?"

"Oh, yeah. Thanks oodles."

"You should go back to sleep."

"I wasn't sleeping."

He rested his hand on my shoulder, stroking his thumb across the deep scar on my neck.

"Are we still fighting?"

"No," I sighed. "I don't have the energy to stay mad very long these days."

"Here," he said. "Sit up. I'll help you get rid of this."

I let him pull me forward and slide the other sleeve of the nightshirt off.

"Short sleeves are easier," he decreed. "You should wear the white one."

"Whatever."

"I'll get it," he said, but instead of getting it, he rested his hand on my shoulder again, and we sat that way for a while. I pulled the sheet up to cover my chest, but he folded it back to my waist again.

"Scientific studies reveal," he pretended to read it from a medical journal, "chemotherapy has no effect on tattoo art."

"I'm glad I have it. It's the only part of me that still looks . . ."

"Pretty."

I nodded. Gary moved his hand to my tatoo, covered it for a moment with his palm, then traced with his index finger the opening rose and tendrils and vine that traveled around my nipple.

"Please, don't do that," I tried to tell him over the lump in my throat.

He leaned down and retraced the same path with his tongue.

"Gary . . ." I tried to breathe, " . . . please . . ."

He moved his mouth to my face and caught the tear that slid back sideways from the corner of my eye, kissing downward across my cheeks and lips and wounded neck, back to the wild rose again, and down. We shifted, experimented, compensated. Feasting on each other was one of our favorite ways, and I whispered to him that I wanted that now. When he moved to make that be, I tried to breathe him in. Chemo had begun to take away my olfactory senses; I could barely smell anything anymore, but Gary tasted the same as ever. My mouth was familiar with the full feeling of him pushing against my inner cheek and soft palette. I opened my legs wider to invite him, raising my hips up toward his face, pulling his hips down toward mine, but after only a brief moment, his beard and mustache tickled across the inside of my thigh instead. I sucked harder, as if that would pull his own mouth back to the center, but he pulled away from me completely and lay back on the bed, whispering to me to crawl on top of him, holding the pump in front of my body so as not to tangle the tether. It chirped and whirred again as he laid it on his stomach, and I settled myself in another of our favorite ways, with my feet tucked against his ribcage, my hands resting on the damp grizzly bear fur of his chest.

"Is it too deep?" he asked. "Do you need to stop?"

"No, it's good."

"Then why are you crying?"

"Because I miss you."

"I know. I'm sorry."

"Don't be sorry," I said. "None of this is your fault."

"It's not yours, either."

I shook my head, not to agree or to disagree, only to not talk about it anymore. We stroked and whispered, moving, making love for a long while.

"Stop for a minute," Gary finally breathed.

"No . . ."

"You have to hold still for a minute . . ."

"No . . . go ahead . . . it's all right . . ."

"I want you to come first . . ."

"I'm so tired . . . I don't think I can. But it's okay . . . it's good . . . I just want you to . . . just let me . . . let me feel like I can still give you something . . . ."

I kept whispering to him. Over the years, I've learned to talk and make promises and describe his own intimate workings to him in such a way that makes them come true almost immediately. I reluctantly let him slip out from me, shifted so I could take him in my mouth again, slid my tongue around the graceful ridge and down the sleek underside, but instead of tasting the pleasant fullness against the back of my throat, I suddenly gagged and recoiled.

"*Oh God!*" I coughed. "*Oh my God!*"

"What?" Gary bolted off the bed and caught me in his arms as I staggered away toward the bathroom. "What's wrong?"

"You know what's wrong! You can taste it! I taste like Adria!" I tried to wipe the bitterness away with the back of my hand.

"No—it doesn't—it's okay—"

"I can taste it on you! That came from *inside* me! Why didn't you say something? Why didn't you tell me I taste like *poison?*"

"Shhh . . . you don't . . . you don't." He hugged me harder than I could struggle, pressing the IV pump painfully between our breastbones. "Everything is starting to taste weird to you right now, that's all. Ro said that might happen, remember? It's okay."

"No, it's not. You should have told me." I started crying again. "You can smell it on me . . . you can taste it . . . you should have told me I taste like poison. . . ."

"Shhh . . . you don't. . . ." Gary kissed my face and forehead and pulled me back toward the bed, sitting on the corner, pulling me on his lap, drawing my knees back toward his hips, nestling inside me again. "Shhh . . . c'mon . . . it's okay. . . ."

The sweat on his neck still tasted like his own sweet, salty self, but I could smell the faint chemical tang of Adria on his face. The pump chirped and whirred. I closed my eyes and listened to the chemical enter my veins, polluting my sweat, tainting the silk between my legs, permeating me with a toxic stench that spilled over onto Gary with every stroke.

"Shhhh," Gary was still hushing and kissing. "You're okay . . . you're okay."

"You can smell it on me . . . the clinic . . . the tape and the tubes and the chemicals . . . and sick people . . . Sarah and Sheila—"

"No! You don't think about them. There's nothing you can do for them now. They're gone. All you can do is keep going forward."

"Gary, I look around there, and everybody's *dying*."

"Then don't look around. You look straight ahead." He took my face between his hands and forced my eyes to focus on his. "You look *here*."

"Sarah started chemo the same day I did—Sheila had a little boy just Jerusha's age—"

"*Here!* You keep looking *right here*."

"I don't want to be poisonous to you, Gary. That was the last good part of me. Now everything's gone."

"I'm not." He pulled my hips close against his, pushing deeper inside me. "I'm not gone."

$\mathcal{P}$lum wine. That's the only thing I could think of that had the same sensual essence as the taste of my secret self. In a novel I read a long time ago, a character reacted to her first taste of a woman's "nether region" saying, "Gentle reader, it was not nice." But I was nice. I don't know if this makes me a lesbian or a narcissist, but that private plum wine musk as I've tasted it on a man's mouth, on his "nether region," on his and my own hands—gentle reader, I found it exceedingly . . . nice. It grieved me greatly that my love canal was now more like Love Canal.

That killed it for me.

I'd done it when I was tired. I'd done it when I was stuffy-headed and sneezing. Neither rain nor sleet nor splitting headache nor herniated disc could have stayed me once, but I couldn't get past the idea that this sacred, private part of me was noxious now, that Gary would come away from me not comforted, but contaminated. Every time I heard the word *cancer*, I felt like a dirty ashtray. I found myself constantly putting my hand to my neck, covering the misshapen healing of the biopsy incision. The rotten spot.

Eventually, my senses of taste and smell completely disappeared, leaving a constant metallic tinge that lingered like the phantom itch in an amputated limb. It left me paranoid that I was reeking of chemo wherever I went. A positively Anita Bryant prudishness came over me. I wouldn't allow Gary to kiss me on the mouth or come in contact with any other endothelial part of my body. I dragged him into Victoria's Secret and made him sniff cards spritzed with various scents until he found one called Wild Juniper and Herb, that vaguely reminded him of the healthy me. I secretly bought a bottle of plum wine, but it tasted like quinine. Everything tasted like quinine. Everything smelled like Clorox.

*M*y sister Janis has what she calls the Theory of Fifty. She asserts everyone gets a score of 50 for their life, whether they get it from averaging 49s and 51s or from averaging zeros and hundreds. Eventually, it all evens out. Being a person of passionate nature, I tend to ride a roller coaster between single digits and high nineties. I believe passion is a basic human need, a thing we all sell our souls for at some point, whether it is to be passionately in love or passionately pissed off. (Sometimes the absence of the former leads to the presence of the latter.) Some people like to be angry all the time, but I had always preferred to fill my passion quota with sex.

I paced like a bear at the zoo while Gary took a shower every morning. I tried old tricks I used to use when I was dieting; thinking how icky food really was, how I really didn't want it. It didn't work then, either. No matter how hard I had tried to see a hot fudge sundae as a piece of foam rubber with swamp sludge on it, my visceral self still hungered for it. And no matter how hard I tried now to see Gary's penis as a flaccid kielbasa rooted to a sack of old lady's elbow skin, my visceral self knew that naughtiness Nirvana lay beyond those BVD boxers.

"One of the secrets to personal success," Napoleon Hill wrote in *Think and Grow Rich!,* "is the harnessing of one's sexual energy."

In her poem "Dear Keats," Erica Jong wrote,

Since flesh can't stay
we keep the breath aloft.
Since flesh can't stay,
we pass the words along.

So a few months into chemo, I packed up all this erotic potential and took it to the secret world I had created in my book. The setting was Helena, Montana, as I knew it in my youth, when the altitude did something to my brain and the music did something to my soul. This was the scene of my sexual self-discovery, and to revisit that feeling gave me back a bit of a former self who was young and unafraid and completely at the mercy of the hormone du jour.

I returned to passages I'd originally typed in the hedging presence of my old mental censors (mainly my mother and Sister Mary Corinne, a comp and lit professor at the Catholic college I attended) and rewrote them with monkey-spanking abandon. Mac and Tulsa, the protagonists in my alternate universe, became the happy recipients of all the sex I wasn't getting in the real world, every intimate encounter cooked to perfection in the convection oven of my frustration.

I borrowed Gary's eyes—deep brown eyes, filled with a

history and feeling that drew me into his life the first moment we met—and gave them as a gift to Mac. To Tulsa, I gave my body, imperfect as it was, allowing her the kind of orgasms that used to make my ears ring. I let her smell coffee and mountains on her lover's body, let him taste the sweet plum wine on hers.

Later, the skirmishes were toned down significantly for publication, but the *Orlando Sentinel* still credited me with "unconventional love scenes that scorch the pages." The *Dallas Morning News* said something about "sparks flying on impact."

"Joni Rodgers can write sex scenes that'll make your toes curl and your hair stand on end," Pam Houston generously said in a cover blurb.

Little did they know that, before the sleepless midnight hours of chemo, this book was about as torrid as *The Bobsy Twins at the Seashore*.

But my poor Gar Bear. He's not into literary friction. Without a secret world of his own, he ended up having a serious spike of high blood pressure.

That passion, I tell ya. It's some powerful stuff.

6

Daughters of the Pioneers

A woman has no reflection so pristine as her mother; no stronger ally, no greater enemy—except perhaps, herself.

—ALEXANDRA FIRESTEIN

I want my daughter to know that cancer doesn't run in our family. Badlands do.

My great-great-grandmother, Lillian Isabelle, was a pioneer. She agreed to marry and go west with a man named T. T. Armstrong, but on her arrival in eastern Montana, she discovered T. T. stood for "Twelve Toes," and he already had an Indian wife and several children living in the dugout that stood in place of the house he'd promised her. The Indian wife threatened to kill her if she didn't leave, but it was imperative that T. T.'s family be perceived as white in order to legally maintain the homestead, and Lillian was already pregnant.

Her daughter, Lucy Armstrong, was called Little Blue Cloud and grew up speaking the Native American language, but a gentle gentleman, Bailey Fisher, civilized her somewhat. She was a writer and a circuit-riding justice of the peace—an unheard of occupation for a woman of her day—and she had a baby with only the help of her little daughter, Stella.

Stella was a born caregiver, and perhaps that's what made her stay with Leonard Smith, a cowboy musician who was sometimes wonderful, but many times abusive and other times just plain gone. They lived on a ranch in the Badlands above a town called Wheeler, and their daughter, my mother, Lois Smith rode her pony to the reservation school where girls beat each other up and pierced their own ears using a needle, a potato, and a piece of ice.

My mother was a cowgirl with an artist's heart, and then she was a waitress, on her own at sixteen in the enormous city of Fargo, and then she was a traveling musician, living in a tiny trailer (and occasionally the car) with her eighteen-year-old husband, Del. He went into radio, and they moved to the Midwest, still playing gigs, but leading, for the most part, a conventional life, adding Allen, Linda, Diana, Janis, and finally me and my little brother, Roger, to their musical act and pleasant suburban lifestyle.

I grew up singing gospel harmony with my sisters, listening to bluegrass, Beatles, and Broadway musical soundtracks. When I was four, Diana taught me how to read from her Betty and Veronica comic books as we whispered and hid after bedtime in the glow of the bathroom night light. I went to parochial school and read all the Narnia Chronicles the summer between fourth and fifth grade. I got my first period when I was eleven and wrote my first song with my best friend, Denine, when we were both twelve. I never could do a cartwheel or open my fingers into Spock's "live long and prosper" gesture, but I was always very good at jacks. And skipping rope. And singing. I was always singing.

These are things I want my daughter to know about me.
I wouldn't exactly call myself a pioneer, but I'd like for
her to think I stood my place in the line of strong women
from which she came.

I want my daughter to know that,
in July of 1987, I won a Montana State Broadcasting Associ-
ation Award for Best Large Market Program. To my knowledge, I was one of the first women to win that award, one of
the first women in the city to hold a full-time air shift on any
radio station, blazing my own little footpath, if not exactly a
trail.

It wasn't what I set out to do. I originally wanted to be a
minister, believe it or not. But I was raised a Wisconsin Synod
Lutheran, so my brother went off to seminary, while I and
the rest of God's least-favorite gender were encouraged to
teach kindergarten and clean the parsonage. Then I wanted
to be an actor, but after I partied myself out of the swanky
liberal arts college I'd scholarshipped myself into, the hinter-
lands beckoned. I crashed out to Montana and, to make a
long story slightly less interminable, begged, badgered, and
wheedled my way into a job at a Helena radio station.

By the late seventies, women had made important
inroads into the male-dominated world of broadcasting all
over the country, but in Helena—well, let me remind you of
an old joke about a newspaper headline reading, WORLD
ENDS: TREND EXPECTED TO REACH MONTANA IN TEN YEARS.

My own father, who was the general manager of a radio
station in Wisconsin at the time, told me the female voice was
incompatible with the airwaves. Various program directors at
Helena stations echoed that sentiment and repeatedly told me
they'd never had a girl on the air full-time, and there were a

lot of other people in line ahead of me, so not to get my hopes up and so forth, but I was determined to convince one particular guy I could do the job. I'd already studied for and acquired my license on my own, so he finally agreed to let me hang out and "observe" (without pay, of course) during his air shift. This entailed getting his coffee, running his production dubs, and pushing buttons to segue between songs while he was on the phone with groupies or in his office snorting cocaine. I was polite and competent. I was eager and inventive. I was conscientious and thorough. But what won him over in the end? I was available.

The night his graveyard-shift announcer quit, and I was the only person he could get on two hours' notice, this young man suddenly saw the light of feminist truth. It didn't hurt that he also had a party to go to. He offered me a starting salary of six hundred dollars a month, and I knew I had hit the big time.

As the clock ticked toward midnight, the control board stretched out in front of me like the cockpit of a 747, and I was ready to fly. I settled my first album on the turntable and waited through the news outro.

I hit the Start button.

I umm . . . I—I hit the Start button. . . .

I hit the Start button!

START! START! START!

Nothing. Silence. Dead air, as they say in the biz.

Radio silence is a little understood but greatly feared phenomenon. It's a longer, deeper, more silent silence than regular silence. Regular silence is simply the absence of sound. Radio silence is the *presence* of the absence of sound. As the result of a panic-induced quantum flux in the time-space continuum, three seconds of radio silence translate into approximately two and a half hours of agonized real time.

I started thrashing at the dials, meters, and potentiometers. I jammed carts in the cart deck and pushed every green button I laid my eyes on. Then I did something that in all my years in the ol' air chair, I never did again.

I said, "Shit!"

Truly, it was barely a whisper. Nay, a peep! Less than a *murmur.*

Okay, it was more like a croak. A huge, glottal croak. And it came audibly and distinctly back to me in my headphones. This was, of course, the moment I realized that instead of turning up the turntable, I'd turned up the microphone.

Not the debut I'd dreamed of. But *woo-hoo!* I was finally on the air!

By the next morning, having struggled through to the end of the shift, I was finally beginning to feel I had my feet under me. Just before 6:00 A.M.—just inches from a clean getaway—the very last thing I had to do was give a public service announcement:

"The United Singles will have their next meeting May first."

"*How does it feel . . . to be on your own?*" Bob Dylan queried, as I practiced the PSA in my most announcerly voice at least fifty times.

"The United Singles will have their next meeting May first. The United Singles will have their next meeting May first . . . ."

Then I opened my mike and said, "The United Singles will have their next mating, me first!"

O̲ver the years, I moved on to larger markets but ultimately returned to Helena for a prime drive-time air shift. Eventually, I won the grudging respect and, in some cases, even the friendship of my fellows there, and I'd like to think I helped open doors for other women who came after me. I'd also like to think I did it all through sharp wit and outrageous moxie, but the truth is it was a little dumb luck combined with a lot of what a mule does on its way out of the Grand Canyon. Lacking any genitals shaped like a microphone, I had to work twice as hard as my compadres just to prove I had a right to be there. I had to keep my mouth shut when doing so practically burst blood vessels in my head. I had to laugh at the good-ol'-boy humor during jock meetings and pretend I wasn't offended by the gigantic T&A poster on the back of the control-room door. I had to clean the toilet and make coffee and do the garbage production until I convinced them I was not leaving, no matter what they said or did to me. But little by little, I proved myself as an announcer, a producer, and a good ol' boy.

And I loved my job.

It perfectly complimented (and subsidized) my theater habit and kept my voice in great shape. The air name gave me someone to *be*, and provided me with a steady supply of the same positive reinforcement I'd grown up with. From the time I was a six-year-old, singing "One-Eyed, One-Horned Flying Purple People Eater" onstage at the Rotary convention, applause has always been my narcotic of choice. Inevitably, I got too old to be cute, however, and there was a long dry spell. Then I stepped out onto the airwaves and discovered that being invisible was even more powerful than being beautiful. Sitting unseen, I discovered the aphrodisiacal quality of mystery. My phone rang off the hook with flattering offers and indecent proposals that would never have been made to my plain face. Who wouldn't wallow in that like Demi Moore on a mattress full of money?

Before Jay Leno was famous enough to leave the small-town stand-up circuit behind, but after he'd been on Letterman a few times, I had occasion to interview him, and he said, "Entertaining is the cushiest job in the world. How many jobs are there where people constantly tell you how great you are? Most people don't have a boss who applauds them at the end of the day and says, 'Yeah! You're terrific! And thank you for coming to work today!'"

Seven years after my nefarious debut, the station's sales manager accepted the Best Program award on my behalf and quipped, "This is the second most exciting thing to happen to her this week."

I'd spent the gala evening in the hospital, breathing toward the birth of my baby boy.

*M*alachi Blackstone Rodgers—Ike for short—was named after an Old Testament prophet and Gary's sea-captain ancestor. Four weeks overdue and weighing in at almost ten pounds, he was born at twenty minutes after twelve midnight in the middle of a thunderstorm. He inherited Gary's brown eyes and my eagerness to laugh, and he rewrote the universe as we knew it.

When Dr. Donaldson drew him out of me after two hours of pushing, my baby was bruised and disgruntled, his poor little noggin squashed and elongated from the long delivery. He didn't cry, he sort of *harrumphed*.

"What are we supposed to call this boy?" Dr. D. asked the proud papa who'd dutifully stood stirrupside the whole time.

Gary took our little alien in his arms and tenderly said, "We were thinking something Biblical, but he actually looks more like . . . Beldar Conehead."

I had planned what I thought was an excessive three months off, but as the end of my maternity leave drew closer, I knew I couldn't go back. Flying in the face of all that was won for me by my feminist foremothers, completely square and politically incorrect, I chose to bag my career in broadcasting and join an endangered species: I became a full-time, stay-at-home, spit-up shouldered, up-to-the-elbows-in-diapers-and-Dr. Seuss mommy.

My friends were mortified. This was after Betty Friedan and before *thirtysomething*, so having children had not yet come back into vogue.

"How can you waste your talent and intelligence scrubbing floors and mashing bananas?" they asked.

"You'll be back," my boss intoned. "I give it six months."

Six months later, I was expecting another baby. Another boy, ultrasounds indicated, and we named him Hannibal after the grand fellow who rode an elephant over the alps. We celebrated. Made plans. I gave Gary a white China elephant for Christmas, and we installed a second crib in the nursery.

It's too painful and private for me to say anything more than that Hannibal died before he was born. But I often dream of elephants to this day.

Unwilling to face that kind of pain again, I went in eight weeks later to get my tubes tied, only to discover I was expecting again. Gary and I struggled to decide whether we should terminate the pregnancy, which was fraught with problems. Placenta previa was immediately apparent. The bleeding increased, my water broke, and I went into labor only four months later, but my daughter was determined to become a citizen of the planet Earth. She was born on St.

Patrick's Day at twenty minutes after twelve noon in the middle of a blizzard.

Jerusha Isabelle—aka Rudy, aka Tooty, aka JuJuBee, Miss My, Pita Pocket, and Jim-jiminy Jim-jim-jeru—was named for a Michener heroine and my pioneering great-great-grandma. She inherited my penchant for melodrama and (God bless her) Gary's munificent nose. She pulled me into the future with her perfect voice and beautiful woman-to-be body, and her birth ushered in a two-year tornado of exhaustion and bliss; laundry, lullabies, and first times for everything. My days became a joyful blur of domestic hyperdrive; I was Donna Reed in the Twilight Zone.

Put breakfast on the table. Clean breakfast off the floor. *Can you tell me how to get, how to get to* Sesame Street? "Mommy!" "Next time, use the potty, okay?" Put lunch on the table. Clean lunch off the floor. Nap time (not for me, unfortunately). "Get your crayons while I rock the baby." Scrub crayons off wallpaper. "Hi, Honey, what's for supper?" Get supper on the table. Clean supper off the floor. "You do him in the bathtub while I do her in the sink." Read *The Sneetches and Other Stories* with a variety of funny character voices (after all, I'm a professional). "Now I lay me down to sleep, I pray the Lord my soul to keep." (Gary and I eighty-sixed the "If I should die before I wake" part. I didn't want to give God any ideas.) Kisses. Sweet sleepyheads. Doze on the couch until the baby starts crying. Diarrhea and diaper rash. "Mommy!" Bad dream. (Is the kid having one or am I?) I am: the baby has more diarrhea. Put bedding in the laundry, lay down on the floor. "Mommy! Can I have hummy-nut Cheerios for breakfast?" Put breakfast on the table . . . clean breakfast off the floor. *It's a beautiful day in the neighborhood.* . . .

I was happy, but I was working awfully hard at it. There were never enough hours in the day, and no matter how much I did, it was never enough for me. My own mother had stayed home to raise her six children, but at the same time, she wrote for local newspapers, developed her own pictures in a basement darkroom, learned to fly the two-seat Aronca Champ she and Dad bought, and still managed to sew new dresses for all four of her daughters every Christmas and Easter. A tough act to follow.

Nineteen ninety-four was going to be my year.

We moved to Houston, Jerusha went off to kindergarten, and things started happening quickly. I signed with a large talent agency and immediately got a commercial and several auditions. I was optimistically working on my manuscript, originally titled *MacPeters' Midlife Crisis*, but now called *Last Chance Gulch*, having received numerous encouraging rejection letters (as opposed to form rejection letters) from publishers and agents. It seemed that everything I'd planned to do "someday when both the kids are in school" was about to come to fruition. I was about to make the leap back into real life, butterflying from a cocoon of part-time dabbling to become a full-time human being again.

When I was diagnosed with cancer less than three months later, I tasted a flash of raw, hard bitterness. I was about to disappear from the earth, and I'd wasted the last seven years of my life scrubbing floors and mashing bananas.

Someone once asked Dr. Wendy Harpham, "When are children old enough to be told a parent has cancer?" Her wise reply: "As soon as they're old enough to be told 'I love you.'"

So, even though several people advised us not to, Gary

and I sat our children down at the dining room table and told them everything. They were only five and seven years old, but they were a precocious five and seven, not easily fooled by the usual parental prevarication. They already knew something was up, and I knew that if we didn't tell them what was going on, they would only be certain of two things: (1) something was terribly wrong at our house, and (2) nobody was telling the truth about it. Better to have them know that, among life's uncertainties, they could always count on a straight answer to any question they needed to ask.

"Well," I started, a little shaky but determined to blurt it all out. "As you know things have been very weird around here lately, and I had to have this operation called a biopsy."

"The biopsy is a test they do in order to figure out if a person has a sickness called cancer," Gary took over. "And Mom does. She does have cancer."

He described the way our bodies are made up of millions of tiny cells that fit together like Legos, each one with a special job to do. Then he drew a little diagram of a cell and scribbled it out to show it getting all yucky and explained how cancer is when the cells get sick and grow wrong. When that didn't seem to be sinking in, we used a little analogy suggested by Gary's mother, who'd gone through chemo for breast cancer several years earlier.

"Pretend Mom is a garden, and there are these weeds, see . . . and you have to kill the weeds before they kill the flowers, right?"

"Can't you just pull the weeds?" Jerusha piped up.

"Well . . . no," Gary said. "Because . . . these weeds are—they're really, really bad weeds, and there's too many of them."

"But some weeds are pretty. Some weeds are good weeds."

"Well, these aren't good weeds. They're bad."

"Dandelions are weeds, and they're pretty. Maybe Mom's weeds are—"

"Okay, forget the weeds." Gary was getting exasperated. "Think about . . . umm . . ." He looked over at me as if to say, "You're the one who wants to be a writer. *Think* of something!"

"Jerusha, it's like . . . what if there was a . . . a delicious golden apple and . . . hmm." I made a conscious decision to drop the metaphors. "Okay. I'm not really like an apple, and cancer isn't like . . . I guess it's not really like anything. It's just . . . cancer. It's a very bad disease. It's making some of the cells in my body grow weird, and if they keep on growing weird, I could get really, really sick. So Dr. Ro is going to give me some very powerful medicine to make it go away. But the medicine is so powerful, it kills a lot of my good cells right along with those bad cells. So it might seem like it's making me sick, even though it's actually making the cancer go away."

We sat and talked for a long time. They didn't cry. They didn't seem to be afraid, and I wondered if they had any understanding of what they were being told.

Later that same day, we took them to H & H Ranch for the airline's company picnic. The founders of the feast had outdone themselves with camel and pony rides, a Ferris wheel, the Scrambler, and other carnival scream machines, even bungee jumping. Ike and Rudy roamed this wonderland with their enormous webby towers of cotton candy, wanting me to go with them on everything. This had suddenly become an incredibly important day, and the significance of it was not lost on them. They might not have understood the particulars of cellular biology, but they felt us drawing together. They sensed we were gathering our forces like the Swiss Family Robinson as pirates neared the perimeter of their island paradise.

As we walked, I was taken in by the beauty of every movement they made. I knew their bodies better than I knew my own. I was their constant caregiver, calculating their temperatures to a tenth of a degree with the palm of my right hand. I was their Aristotelian tutor, unlocking the secret world of words with refrigerator magnet letters. I was their champion, marching up to the neighborhood bully's front door; their advocate, polite but firm in the face of the gargantuan grade-school principal.

Watching them that day, I was overwhelmed with the privilege it is to parent another human being, the luxury of love, the decadence of caring. Not one day of their existence had passed that I wasn't with them, not one day had I wasted by replacing them in priority with something so fleeting and insubstantial as a touring show or a radio commercial. I loved both radio and theater, but when I disappeared from that plane of existence, I hardly left a blank space. This was the one thing in the world only I could have done. And I did it as well as I could.

It gave me some peace to know that, come what may, while they had me, they really had me.

We made jokes about it when my hair went away. We let them watch with gruesome fascination as Gary changed the dressing on my cath port site. We answered their questions with unflinching honesty and searched in vain for books and video resources that might help them make sense of it all. We told them over and over again that everything would be all right, but there's no way you can convince a child that mommies are allowed to nap all afternoon and then go to bed at eight. Mothers are not supposed to cry. Mothers are not supposed to throw up.

"Mommy!" Jerusha would wail from outside the bathroom, and if I didn't answer, she would kick the doorjamb and shout, "Joni Rodgers! You stop that!" And when I couldn't stop, she would sit there and cry.

We tried various diversionary tactics to get her to go away, but nothing would budge her. Then one day, it dawned on me that this was a Badlands woman outside my bathroom door. She was as brave as Lillian Isabelle, as caring as Stella Fisher. To tell her she was helpless and ask her to walk away from a loved one who was in pain—that was asking her to go against her biology. I finally opened the door, let her sit beside me, and asked her to soak a washcloth in cold water. As long as she was there, holding it against my forehead, she wasn't afraid.

Since Jerusha was in half-day kindergarten, and our after-school child-care options were limited by both crumbling finances and the small number of acquaintances I'd made in our new hometown, we had no choice but to take her downtown with us for many of the chemo treatments. She charmed the scrubs off the staff wherever we went: Dr. Ro's office, the chemo clinic, the pharmacy, and the phlebotomist's lab. She was fascinated by the strange procedures and props used by the doctors and nurses and asked a thousand questions, as insatiably curious as Kipling's baby elephant.

"That's heparin," she informed a nurse one day (though I'm hoping the nurse knew this already, since she was injecting it into my cath port). "It prevents blood from clotting."

"That's right!" The nurse was duly impressed. "Are you going to be a doctor when you grow up?"

"No," Jerusha said. "I'm going to be a single comedian."

There was generous laughter all around, as if to help get her career started.

"Do you help take care of your mommy?" another nurse asked her.

"Yes," Jerusha proudly informed her. "I'm her fashion coordinator."

"Oh?"

"Yeah. I used to be her beautician. I brushed her hair, and I braided her hair. And—do you know what a snood is?"

"Hmm," the nurse thought on it for a moment. "Is it like a bow with a pouch under it, and you put your ponytail in the pouch so it makes a bun?"

"Uh-huh. Like a ballerina Barbie's bun. And I even *snooded* my mom's hair. But now, she said I could be her fashion coordinator, which is better because that's the whole person instead of just on top of their head."

"Ah, I see." The nurse nodded, understanding completely. She finished the Heparin push and squeezed my hand. "You look very fashionably coordinated, Mom. Somebody's doing a good job."

The secret to keeping this thing from ripping Jerusha's world apart, I discovered, was to make it part of her world. To give her an active role to play and respect her need to play it.

My mother was the very same way.

As the diagnostic process funneled closer and closer to its inevitable conclusion, I tried to prepare her, but the day I actually had to speak the words, I recognized the gaping wound I was leaving on her heart.

"I'm sorry," she told me. "I shouldn't be crying when here you are in the middle of your worst nightmare."

"Mom, I'm not in the middle of my worst nightmare," I replied. "I'm in the middle of *your* worst nightmare."

She was the one whose daughter was dying. I wouldn't

have changed places with her for the world. And she would have given the world to change places with me.

Of course, she wanted to fly down immediately, but it was mutually decided that she should wait until my chemo was under way. She could take only a certain amount of time off from her job at the newspaper in Helena, and we figured I'd really need the help a little further down the line. We figured right. She came alone (it was also mutually decided that Dad could just as effectively pace the floor and whistle nervously at their own house) and brought me her mandolin, because she knew it was difficult for me to play guitar with the longline in my arm.

That night, she tucked the kids in bed, cleaned up the supper dishes, and picked toys up from the living room floor. Finally, she made tea for the two of us, serving mine to me on the couch.

"Wow, having kids sure is a lot of work," I smiled wanly. "I can't wait until they're all grown up and don't need me anymore."

"Yes," Mom smiled back, then nodded toward my teacup. "Is it too strong?"

"No, it's fine. It's just—I get these sores in my mouth, and now they're spreading down my throat. It's kind of hard to swallow."

Mom rocked in the rocking chair, sipping her tea. We talked and laughed until after midnight, even though she kept saying I should go to bed. I didn't want the day to end; I was so glad to see her again. Sometimes, when I was in Helena teaching theatre school for weeks at a stretch, we'd start grinding on each other a bit. In addition to our widely divergent political and spiritual convictions, my mom is a person who needs her peace, and I'm a person who can't keep my mouth shut. The combination sometimes got a little inflammatory. But there was no trace of that now.

"You can take that off if you want to," she said, referring to my white linen headwrap.

"No, it's fine."

"Well, you keep scratching under it. It must be uncomfortable."

"It is a little, but . . ."

"It's all right," she assured me, and I realized she probably wanted to see what it looked like, the way I would say, "Oh, show me, sweetie," if Jerusha came running to me with her latest boo-boo.

"It's actually kind of comical," I shrugged and unwrapped the turban instead of pulling it off all at once. "It actually looks pretty funny."

She didn't appear to get the joke. I did a few of my standard one-liners, but she still didn't laugh. I felt guiltier than I did several years earlier when she found out I'd tried to tempt my little brother into smoking grass.

She asked about the schedule for the week, and I told her about a lung function test, MUGA scan, and the next round of chemo.

"I just know God is going to heal you," she said in a way that made me certain she believed I was dying.

*T*here were two days between Mom's arrival and my next dose of chemo, and we were determined to use that time to show her some of the sights of Houston. I suggested the Museum of Fine Arts, but Jerusha begged for the Museum of Natural History, and it was hard to refuse. We drove down into the city the next morning, bought our tickets, and entered the towering rain-forest environment of the museum's Cockerel Butterfly Center. I'd been feeling relatively okay till then, but wandering through the hot, misty jungle, I started feeling weak and light-headed. I sat down on a bench, but it was getting harder to separate the roar of the waterfall from the rushing in my head.

"Are you all right?" Mom kept asking, and I kept saying, "Sure. Fine."

Pioneer women don't whine.

We walked past the dinosaurs and seashells. We rode the Geovator that pretends to go down into an oil well and strolled the extensive geological displays (which I'm sure have nothing to do with extensive funding from the petroleum industry, environmentally conscious lovers of art and culture that they are). We came to the maze of precious stones, and I told Mom and Jerusha to go on without me.

"Are you sure you're all right?" Mom asked.

"Sure. Fine. But I think I'll wait here," I added, sitting on a bench near the exhibit.

Mom took Jerusha's hand, looking back over her shoulder only once before they disappeared into the dusky half-light of the treasure cave. I didn't realize how sleepy I was until I awoke to the sound of Mom's voice beside me. She was telling Jerusha about the Badlands, about the camping expeditions with her brother and sister, about her parents' agate shop. (I vaguely remember them making gloriously gaudy lamps, bolo ties, and belt buckles about as big as your head.)

"Do they still own their agate shop?" Jerusha asked.

"No. My father died a long time ago." She didn't mention he'd succumbed to the same disease that had skipped a generation and settled on me. "And my mother died when you were just a baby."

"Oh, poor Grandma." Jerusha touched her face with genuine sympathy. "That's the saddest thing in the world—to have your mother die."

No, the thought came to my mother and me in unison, *that's not the saddest thing.*

"Are you two ready to go?" I asked, avoiding her eyes.

"Mama!" Jerusha delighted. "You woke up! I'm hungry."

*M*om loved Dr. Ro, which was no surprise. Seeing the two of them side by side, I realized how much they reminded me of each other. Both are diminutive in stature, delicate as spun steel. They're both genteel and soft-spoken, but their meaning can seldom be misunderstood and almost never disregarded. I wondered what in Dr. Ro's childhood in the Far East could have had the same effect as the western desolation of those beautiful, relentless Badlands.

"She is tolerating the chemo very well," Dr. Ro told Mom in a parent-teacher conference sort of way, and Mom nodded, and they both beamed at me.

The inside of my mouth was so full of sores, even a soft slice of Wonder Bread chewed like shrapnel. My stomach was perpetually on the queasy eve of destruction, and just a few days earlier, several of my toenails—which were now striated Pepto pink and Barney-butt purple—had fallen off in the bathtub. I was tolerating chemo about as well as a teapot tolerates a tidal surge, I thought, but then it occurred to me that at least two people who'd started chemo the same week I had were already dead.

"Yeah," I nodded and beamed back. "Tolerating great here."

After the examination, I went to the lab for blood work,

then waited two hours, only to have someone come and tell me there would be no treatment that day. My white count was too low for another onslaught. Fighting tears of frustration, I collected a supply of steroids and Neupogen syringes from the pharmacy and headed back to the suburbs.

The following week, I was good to go, but on day 5 of the cycle, Gary had to half carry me up the stairs after I received the Bleo booster. I was violently ill, gripped by a searing headache and washed out with fatigue. Gary needed to nap for a while before going to work, so Mom installed me in Jerusha's room, where she could quietly come and go with a clean basin and cool washcloth. When I could bear to open my eyes for a moment, the fear I saw in her face rolled another wave of guilt into the dull ache at the back of my skull. But as painful as it was for my mother to be there, I understood (because I'm a mother, too) that this was where she needed to be. She knew this was going on with or without her, and her being there made it easier for both of us. I could feel the prayers in her cool hands, hear the presence of calm in her soothing voice. I let myself float on it.

"If I should die before I wake . . ."

It actually didn't sound like such a bad idea after all. I could make it all stop if I discontinued my chemo. Everything bad. It could all just stop.

When I opened my eyes, Jerusha was sitting on the floor playing Barbies. I had resolved when my daughter was yet in utero that this wasp-waisted bimbo icon would never cross our threshold, but that lasted about as long as the high-minded "My children will never see anything but public television" proclamation.

My own Barbie was the stiff-limbed Sixties version, with

ice-blue eyeshadow and faint arching brows, but years of hard-core bimbo icon action had burdened her with a host of imperfections. Her ash-brown hair had to be cut off after a wad of Blackjack gum got stuck in it, and a nasty run-in with a Tonka truck had left one of her breasts badly inverted. By the time I passed her on to my daughter, she was as smudgy and abused as a voodoo doll, but for some reason, Jerusha had tenderly selected her from a whole suitcase full of fresh, busty blondes.

"Time for a Bleo booster," Jerusha announced. She laid Barbie out on top of a shoe box lid and tied a string to her arm so Dr. Skipper could administer the treatment.

"She'll be all better soon," I said.

Jerusha came over and laid her small, cool hand on my forehead.

"Do you have to throw up some more?" she asked.

"No, I'm feeling better now."

"I can get the bucket for you."

"That's okay, sweetie. I don't need it right now." I scooched over and patted the bed in front of me. "Wanna cuddle in?"

She held up her finger in an *uno momento, por favor* gesture, then went to a small pink purse Mom had given her and took out a half roll of Wint-o-green LifeSavers.

"How 'bout a little snack first," she suggested diplomatically, slipping one between my lips.

"Oh. Sorry."

She crawled onto the bed and snuggled her back against me, spoon fashion.

"Mom?"

"Hmm."

"Did you ever notice how all the girls in my class are allowed to have nail polish?"

"No. I hadn't noticed that."

"Can I have nail polish?"

"*May* I have nail polish."

"*May* I have nail polish?"

"No."

"Why not?"

"Because." I hoped that would be enough, but she lurched against me to indicate it wasn't. "It creeps me out when I see little girls all dolled up like that."

"Because it makes them look trashy," she quoted me with only a hint of sarcasm.

"That's right."

Rather than argue the point, Jerusha snuggled closer to me and attempted a stealth approach.

"Mom?"

"Hmm."

"A girl can be anything she wants to be, can't she?"

"She sure can. Anything in the world."

"Know what I want to be, Mom?"

"What?"

"All dolled up!"

I laughed, more at myself than at her. Usually, my biases could be conveniently compartmentalized, but this was truly a feminist dilemma. Could I support her right to be an underwater spot welder or astrophysicist without supporting her right to be a bouffant trophy girlfriend or Dallas Cowboy cheerleader if that was her choice?

"Mom, do I have to go home on the bus with Simon again tomorrow?" she asked, saving me from having to work it out for the moment.

"Well, Simon's mom offered, Pinky, and I won't be back from the doctor's office until five or so."

"I hate going home on the bus with Simon," she groaned. "It's fun at his house, but when we get on the bus, everybody says, 'Simon and Jerusha—kissy, kissy, kissy!'"

"I'm sorry, sweetie. But I really don't have anyplace else for you to go. Daddy needs to sleep, and Grandma is taking me to the doctor."

"Can't I come with you?"

"Jelly Bean, you've already missed twenty-nine days of school this year. You need to go."

"You don't care," she sulked. "Nobody ever told you 'kissy, kissy, kissy.'"

"Yes they did."

"In kindergarten?"

"No, in high school. So they were big enough to think of worse stuff than kissy kissy."

"Why did they tease you?" She let go of her own issue in favor of what she hoped would be a good story.

"Because Billy Cato grabbed hold of me and kissed me."

"Where?" She curved in toward me so we could share like girlfriends.

"In the band room. Right in front of the percussion section."

"No," she giggled. "I mean *where?*"

"Right—*smmmmack!*—on the *lips*," I said, giving proper dramatic emphasis to the gory detail, and Jerusha squealed with horror and delight.

"Then what happened?"

"Then suddenly, this bag I was carrying—it was full of my nightgown and underwear and Saturday clothes because I was going to spend the night at my friend's house—the bag just ripped open, and everything fell out on the floor."

"How come it ripped?"

"Well, it might have gotten kind of squashed between us. But I think it was actually because the entire universe suddenly reversed direction on a subatomic level."

Jerusha giggled again. She loves answers like that.

"That's what it felt like?"

"Yup."

"What did you do then?"

"I don't remember."

"Yes, you do!"

"I guess I went in the bathroom and cried for a little while. Then for the whole rest of the school year, I tried to pretend I was Katherine in *The Taming of the Shrew*. The nasty first-act Katherine who's way smarter than all the boys."

Jerusha reached her hand up and stroked my smooth forehead and scalp.

"Mom?"

"Hmm."

"If Simon ever kisses me right smack on the lips, I'm gonna punch his lights out."

"Good girl."

She wriggled onto her back and propped her foot up on my knee, ready for a new topic.

"Grandma made chicken for supper," she informed me.

"Yum," I said, but had to purposely relax my stomach's reaction to the very idea.

"I hate chicken," Jerusha said.

"No, you don't. You love chicken."

"Only Chicken McNuggets."

"Well, I hope you didn't say anything rude to Grandma. I hope you ate it and said it was good."

"Poor Grandma," she sighed, then whispered in confidence, "Her mother died."

I tried to remember what I knew about death when I was five. All I could come up with was a neighbor boy who went off to Vietnam, and then one day, we weren't supposed to ask about him anymore.

Then I tried to remember what I knew about my mother when I was five, but all that came back to me were the images and impressions from earlier that day. Cool hands, calm voice, the presence of love, a quiet but continuous coming and going from my life. Jerusha might retain that much if I died now, but little else. Nothing except I loved her, and then I was gone.

I felt a desolate need to tell her everything she would ever need to know, to warn her about so many things I'd learned the hard way, to reassure her she wasn't going crazy, even when she felt like she was, and let her know she wasn't the first one to feel all those impossible emotions she would inevitably experience. But to say any of this to her now would only frighten her. Could any of us have enjoyed our childhood if we had had an inkling of what it would be to grow up?

Showing someone a map of Pennsylvania in autumn simply can't prepare them for the bitter wind—or the resplendent foliage. It's a trip you have to make for yourself.

Maybe a mom is just a glorified tour guide.

*P*ioneer women don't see shrinks, either, but when a Cancer Counseling Inc. brochure came into my hands, I, being less than the perfect pioneer woman, decided to blaze a trail to their glass-walled office and take advantage of their generous offer to set me up for several sessions free of charge with someone who specialized in treating families coping with cancer.

"Now let me get this straight," Dr. Silverberg said from his gray moderne psychologist's chair. "You're upset because your mother is being nice to you."

"No, it's not that. She's always been nice. We've always had a great relationship. It's just that I used to be the black sheep of the family, you know? It was a little hobby for me. I was the one who left home at eighteen—and not to get married. I was the one who caroused and gave them gray hair and—well, now I can do no wrong. My parents never judged me out loud, but underneath there was always a good solid base of disapproval, and I found that very bracing. Now, all I have to do is keep breathing, and they're satisfied. She doesn't even raise her eyebrows when I cuss. My old flame called me on the phone, and all she said was, 'Oh, how is he doing?'"

"Maybe she doesn't feel those things are worth arguing over in this situation," Silverberg suggested. "Cancer tends to place petty concerns and irritations in a broader context."

"Maybe. But I can only suppose this is what Catholics felt like when the pope told them it was okay to eat meat on Friday, after all. Like you just can't count on anything anymore."

"And you see your mother as being the pope in this scenario?" He wrote something down on his tablet.

"My mother is knockout drop-dead beautiful. She looked like a movie star when she was young, and she only improved with age. She's a brilliant musician. She can play anything with strings, including the piano. She writes, she knows how to fly an airplane and develop pictures in a darkroom, and she's never missed sending out birthday cards and prompt thank-you notes. She's intelligent and kind and the most gracious person I've ever known."

"She sounds like a remarkable woman."

"Can't you see how that would drive a person crazy? I

try to be perfect like her, but I can't. I come from this long line of exceptional women, and I've tried so hard to be exceptional, too—but I'm just not. I haven't accomplished anything, and now I'm afraid my time is running out. They'll feel compelled to make something up. They'll tell Jerusha about her wonderful mother, but it'll be the Disney version of me. Some retouched, glossy, edited-for-family-viewing version of who I really was. Because when you play Barbies, you don't pretend Barbie is this fat, flawed, neurotic, *bald* lady. You pretend she's perfect."

"So . . . in this scenario your mother would be . . . Walt Disney?" Dr. Silverberg said.

"No—she—okay, here's the thing. If I die now, my daughter will only know me from the stories she hears. And no one will say anything bad about me. I can see it starting already. It'll be like Richard Nixon's funeral. They'll make me be this paragon of virtue and maternal sacrifice. I'll be Barbie by the time they get through with me, and I can't do that to her. Do you have any idea how hard it is to feel good about yourself when you have Barbie for a mother?"

"So at the root of your anxiety is the image you'd like to leave behind. You want to control your daughter's perception of you, even after your death."

"I don't want my daughter to be shackled with yester-year's oppressive ideals. I want her to be shackled with *my* oppressive ideals." I listed the principles I hold dear, ticking them off on my fingers. "Rubinesque is beautiful. Our secret family recipe is 'Peel back foil and heat.' Ironing is what happens when you throw the blouse into the dryer with a wet towel. You don't have to shave your legs above the knee, and the eyelash curler is the instrument of the devil."

"Ah. Then you want to control your daughter's perception of *everything*."

"Yes!" I exclaimed. "Doesn't every good mother? But how do I do that?"

"Well, there's only one way," he shrugged, as if slightly irritated to have to state the obvious. "Don't die."

Easier said than done. I didn't say it out loud, but my Adria pump chirped in agreement nonetheless.

*M*om went home. Christmas came. After reading the story of Mary and Joseph, I tucked the kids in, admonishing that Santa wouldn't come if they didn't go to sleep, but they were too excited, so I sat on the floor, singing carols with the mandolin until the sugar plum visions started doing their thing.

In the living room, Gary stared at *It's a Wonderful Life.* I cuddled onto the couch next to him, and he held me hard; not in a death grip, but for dear life. Neither of us made any comment, but we were both watching the old movie with new eyes, recognizing how the whole world really can change for lack of one person who loves and is loved.

Later, as we arranged gifts beneath the tree, I said for the first time that I wanted to discuss how he and the kids would handle it if I didn't survive.

"*Handle* it?" he said incredulously. "There is no *handling* it."

He was right, of course. They were not about to let me go without a fight. No graceful exit was possible. No arrangements or preparations could change the fact that my death would forever alter the landscape of their lives. Their lives would go on, whether or not mine did, but to visualize the healthiest, fullest future for my children, I had to visualize a future that included an imperfect but fully present *me.*

Any doubts I had about continuing chemo dissipated. It

would have been easier to slip away, to accept that nature had selected me for extinction. But my children anchored me to this earth with the possibility that they might go for shaved ice and not spill some on my shoe, that someone else would buy Jerusha her first box of tampons or tell Malachi if he thinks he's going out the door dressed like that he has another think coming. I couldn't bear to have someone else play my role, deliver my lines.

If your friends all decide to jump off a cliff, are you going to do it, too?

Shut that door, we're not air-conditioning the state of Texas!

When I was your age, I had to (insert seemingly impossible task here) *and we didn't even have a* (insert essential element of gracious living) *to take for granted!*

It was my job, my privilege, my honor and duty to say all those things said by every mom, everywhere, every day, every single precious time she's called to action. I was not about to give it up and go gently.

As a woman in training, Jerusha needed me. She would need me no less as an adult than I needed my own mother now, and I would need her no less than my mother now needed me. People I loved stood on either side of me; linking me to the past, drawing me toward morning, and I couldn't bear to break that chain.

How lovely, I thought, *to be so entangled.* And the tears in my eyes turned the Christmas lights into shooting stars and sun dogs.

I wanted more than anything to see who stood just beyond my daughter. Someone with Jerusha's eyes and my voice, my mother's hands and my grandmother's grace, all united with the gentle features of the good men with whom each of us had fallen in love.

7

The Queen Has Cancer

I learn by going where I have to go.
—THEODORE ROETHKE

I don't remember if it was crayons or kickball or what pressing issue of kindergarten politics that prompted my son to pass a poison pen note to his bite-size classmate, but I remember standing in the principal's office, staring at the rumpled construction paper missive.

"DEAR KENNY," it read, "I HATE YOU. YOU BIG BAFOON. MALACHI B. RODGERS."

Malachi had forgotten that (1) you should never put anything like that in writing, and (2) he was the only child in his class who could read. Kenny promptly took the note to the kindergarten teacher, innocently asking her to read it to him, and my boy was instantly up to his ears in hot water, making the first of many hard-earned trips to the principal's office. It didn't help that, when Mrs. Alice called me to report this calumny, I couldn't stop laughing.

"It's not that I condone the passing of unkind notes," I tried to assure her, though my giggles probably made me less credible. "But I mean, c'mon, you've got to admit the use of the word *buffoon* is kind of—I'm sorry. He takes after me, I guess."

"Well," sniffed Mrs. Alice, "perhaps that's not always such a good thing."

I had never for one instant imagined it was.

When I was diagnosed with cancer, two years later (and fifteen hundred miles away from the all-seeing eye of Mrs. Alice), Malachi was a savvy second grader, enrolled in a program for gifted children at his school. He'd seen a lot more television than I had at that point in life and was proficient in the game of Mortal Kombat. He was old enough to know facts but young enough to struggle with implications and smart enough that there was no keeping the truth from him. He accepted with a silent nod each time we explained a new side effect or defined a new clinical term, and I would hear him at night, whispering in the dark, interpreting the foreign tongue for Jerusha.

When a classmate's father was diagnosed with a malignant brain tumor, it was good for both of them to have a friend with whom they could talk about cancer and chemo, but when the other boy's father died just before Christmas, Ike suddenly realized what was at stake.

"Are you going to die, Mom?" he asked me almost nightly after that.

"I'm trying not to," I told him truthfully. "I promise I'll do everything possible to stay here with you as long as I can."

Later, when I wasn't too sure, I started adding something about how he was a part of me and I was part of him because he grew right out of my own body, so no matter what, I would always be with him.

Luckily—or blessedly—probably more by the hand of God than by coincidence—Malachi's second grade teacher was a wonderful lady who'd had Hodgkin's disease more than twenty years earlier. Lagenia Damron had undergone the virulent chemo that set the stage for regimens such as the CHOP+Bleo I was taking, and the wisdom, grace, and beauty with which she emerged from that refining fire provided an important focus for both Malachi and me. Lagenia was like a lighthouse for us that year, telling us merely by standing there that solid ground was within reach.

On a daily basis, she cut Malachi just enough slack to show she cared, but not enough to give him the idea life wasn't going to go on, business as usual. She suggested I come up with a special project for him to work on when he felt especially worried, so I taught him to log on to my computer.

"Now you can be a writer," I told him. "Just like me and Grandma."

"What should I write about?" he asked.

"I don't know. How about dinosaurs?"

"No. Michael Crichton already wrote *Jurassic Park*. That kind of hogged up all the good dinosaur ideas."

"Okay, then how about a superhero who —"

"Lame."

"Oh. Right. Well then . . . "

"I could write a story about cancer."

"If you want to. But it might be more fun to think about something else."

"Nobody around here ever thinks about anything else," he grumbled, and the truth of what he said lay like a stone on the floor between us.

"I know it seems like that sometimes, Spike-man. But it won't always be this way. Meanwhile, how about a story about a little brown bear—"

110

"*Mom.* Wha'd'you think I am—a kindergarten baby?"

"Okay," I was getting exasperated. "A *grizzly* bear, then. One who dismembers and consumes unsuspecting campers in Glacier National Park."

"Geez. That doesn't sound very appropriate for children."

"Here's an idea," I sighed. "I'll go take a nap, and you start working on your story. Then you can surprise me when I wake up, okay?"

Hunting and pecking laboriously, he typed the title extra big.

⌒

THE QUEEN HAS CANCER

Once upon a time . . .

there was a king and queen and prince and princess. Then one day, the queen (the mom) found out she had cancer. Now, not serious cancer, like your grampa might have had/have, but a not so serious cancer.

"Children, gather round," said the queen.

"Yes, mother," said Princess Jerusha.

"Children, I have something called cancer," said the queen.

"What's cancer?" said Princess Jerusha.

"Cancer is a sickness," said King Gary.

"I've heard that people die from that," said Prince Malachi, "The shepherd boy's father had cancer and he died."

"Now, don't talk of such things, I won't die!" said Queen Joni.

"But the shepherd boy's . . ."

"No buts!" said Queen Joni, "I'm not going to die!"

Princess Jerusha was worried and Prince Malachi was shocked. Then Malachi rushed out of the room.

"Blacksmith, make the strongest shield and sword you can," said the Prince. "The strongest in the land! I am going on a long journey to go get the magic moss from the top of a very high mountain."

⁓

A child's life is made up of fragile combinations. The irresistible upward motion of precariously stacked building blocks. The intricate logic of a Tinker Toy Ferris wheel. The smooth symbiosis of peanut butter and jelly.

"Mom . . ."

I awoke to the feeling of a small hand patting on my cheek, but it took me a moment to open my eyes.

"Sweetie, please. Mommy doesn't feel good. Just turn to the Disney channel, okay?"

"But I'm hungry."

"Can you wait till Daddy gets up?"

"I'm *hungry*, Mom."

"Can you make yourself a PB and J?"

"*No*." He seemed startled by the very suggestion. "You have to make it."

"Sweetie, could you just give it a try? C'mon. Be my big boy."

"Why can't you get up and make it? It'll just take a minute. Then you can lay down again."

"All right." I sat up on the couch and dragged my feet to the floor. A wave of nausea and dizziness engulfed me, and I rested my head forward in my hands. "Malachi, I can't. I'm sorry, sweetie, you're going to have to do it yourself."

"Nooooo," he whined, pulling on my arm. "You *know* I don't do that. *You* have to do it."

"Ike, I can't. Do you understand? I want to do it for you, but I can't. You're going to have to do it for yourself or do without."

I lay back down, trying to contain the searing pain behind my closed eyes.

"Mom . . ." The patting resumed.

"Honey, please—"

"Mom, I don't feel good."

"What's the matter?"

"I just don't feel good. I'm sick. Can you get up and make me some—"

"Malachi . . ." I wasn't able to sound nearly as threatening as I would have liked.

"You have to, Mom! I'm too sick. You have to do it."

"You're not too sick, Malachi, you're just too lazy. Now would you please . . . oh . . . Lord . . ." I struggled up from the couch and lurched toward the bathroom.

"Are you going to throw up *again?*" he groaned.

I closed the door behind me. In a little while, I heard the sound of the refrigerator door. Then the silverware drawer. Then a chair scraping across the kitchen floor.

"Mom?" He tapped on the bathroom door. "Should I make one for Jerusha, too?"

"Yes. Thank you, Malachi. That would really help me."

"I'm using more peanut butter than you do. And more jelly."

"Uh-huh."

"Way more."

"Mmm-hmm."

"It'll probably get messy."

"That's okay."

"Mom?" he tapped again.

"What?" My voice reverbed weakly from inside the toilet bowl.

"This is generic peanut butter," he mentioned strictly FYI. "Choosy mothers choose Jif."

⌒

He walked for many days and many nights, taking food and water and a sleeping bag and tent to sleep in.

When it was nighttime, he could hear creatures in the bushes and all kinds of strange noises. Then, the next morning, he went out to hunt for some extra food to eat. Then he saw a huge jack rabbit! He raced at the giant animal and before the jackrabbit could get to his hole, the prince struck him up with his sword. He cooked the rabbit, and ate it that night.

The next morning, he set out on his journey again.

The prince came to a mountain and could not see its peak. He saw smoke and debris all around. A giant dragon emerged from the cave, blowing hot red fire.

⌒

The Fiesta store was always full of music and free samples on Saturday afternoon. A mariachi band strolled the produce department, and Cricket the Clown juggled near the frozen foods. It was the best entertainment we could afford at the time, and we were out of milk and laundry soap, so even though I wasn't feeling so great, I plopped a straw hat on my head and we went over. This was the first cycle of chemo to really hit me hard, and the last cycle I failed to stock up on groceries in advance.

It was that dang turkey bologna that did it to me. A young woman was frying it in an electric skillet, and the peppered meat aroma couldn't be escaped.

"Sample?" she offered as we passed by, holding up a

large, greasy chunk on a toothpick. The moment I saw it, I knew I was going to be sick.

Fortunately, we were close to the ladies' room. I dragged Jerusha inside with me, admonishing Malachi to "stay smack beside that door." He looked at me, wide-eyed; I usually made him come in, too, even though he'd been objecting since he was a burly-man of six.

"I'll guard the cart," he said, inflating the chest of a centurion beneath his Pee-Wee Herman T-shirt. As the door swung shut between us, his face was full of pride and fear.

He struck up his sword and put his shield in front of him. The dragon came forth and charged. And then, his horns threw the shield out into the bushes. The prince came forward, charging with his sword pointed right at the dragon's chest. And then, he missed! The dragon had flown right up!

"Oh, you cowardly dragon! Come back here and fight like a creature!" shouted the prince.

There had been nothing in my stomach since my latest chemo treatment two days earlier, but the dry heaves racked my midsection and resounded embarrassingly within the echo chamber of the public bathroom. When I came out a ten-minute eternity later, Malachi was sitting on the bottom rack of the grocery cart, his eyes filled with tears. A woman was standing over him, and as I opened the door, I heard him tell her, "I'm not supposed to talk to strangers!"

"Are you all right?" she asked me as he rushed to throw his arms around my waist. Southern people are so truly kind. "Is there anything I can do?"

I was never very good at being needy. Like all good pioneer mommy/daughter/sister/PTO/church-volunteer ladies, I was programmed for self-sufficiency and ministry to others, but had a hard time accepting the same help I so cheerfully offered. I hadn't realized yet that ultimate selflessness is ultimately selfish, because it denies others their opportunity to be empowered as ministers.

"No, thank you," I said too bravely. "We'll be okay."

We went to the first available checkout lane, and I gripped the handle of the cart, trying to breathe deeply, struggling to stabilize. By the time the checker was skimming our items across the scanner, I knew I wasn't going to make it.

"I'm sorry," I told her. "I'm not feeling very well."

"It's $36.47," she said, not knowing how else to respond.

"I'm sorry . . ." I blurted again and stumbled over to sit on the ledge at the end of the counter, my head between my knees.

"Ma'am? Ma'am?"

The voices warped and phased through waves of a rushing blackness that engulfed my brain.

"What's the matter with her?"

"I dunno. She's stoned or something."

"No, she looks like she's sick."

"What's that thing on her arm?"

"She has cancer," Malachi said defensively. He had taken charge of the situation and was holding a bag of frozen peas against my head. "That's her chemo pump."

"What's going on?"

I cleared enough to look up at the manager who'd joined the fray.

"It's—it's $36.47," the poor checker repeated helplessly.

"Ma'am, are you all right? Is there someone we can call?"

"No . . . I'm sorry—if I can just get over to the car . . . we just live in the apartment complex across the street. . . ."

I gave Malachi two twenty-dollar bills. He handed them to the checker and collected the change while the manager placed our bags in the cart and wheeled it out to the car.

"Are you sure you're all right?" he kept asking.

"Yes, I'm fine. Thank you."

⌒

Then the dragon, without warning, came shooting down from the sky like a bullet. He blew the biggest batch of fire balls he could. But he missed! Then, the prince came forward with his sword and struck him in the neck!

⌒

"Please help me . . . God, please help me . . ." I begged aloud, trusting the Lord and second nature to guide the keys into the ignition, the clutch into first gear. I was beyond the rational concept that I was in no condition to be driving a car. All I could think about was getting home. I would get home, put the groceries away, make the supper I had planned.

"Mommy, the light is green," Malachi said meekly, and I opened my eyes. We were somehow at the corner now. Someone behind me was honking.

We lurched out into the traffic. More honking as we crept across the traffic lanes, turned into the parking lot of the apartment complex. I suddenly wasn't sure where I was. Malachi and Jerusha were crying in the backseat. I swayed the car over and let it sit, angled across two parking spaces.

"Malachi . . ." I pulled the keys from the ignition and handed them to him. "You have to go get Daddy. Tell him I'm sick. He won't hear you if you knock on the door. You have to open it with the key."

"Mom . . . no . . ."

"Run as fast as you can. Wake him up and tell him I'm sick."

There was more blackness, more dry heaves.

"*Mommy!* Mom, I can't get it open!" Malachi was sobbing. "*Mommy, wake up!* It won't open, Mom! It's stuck!"

I was trying to swim upward toward him, but felt myself sinking instead somewhere beneath heat and darkness and the sound of Jerusha screaming.

The next thing I was aware of was Gary's arm behind my shoulders. Malachi had gone back and asked a neighbor to help him open the door, but Gary was already awake from the frantic pounding and doorbell ringing of Malachi's first effort. He eased me out of the car and up the flight of stairs, laid me on the bed. He called Ro, and she told him to inject me with a white-count booster. He gave me a large pink capsule, but I wasn't able to swallow it.

I slept hard for several hours, and when I was still too weak and dizzy to stand that evening, Gary called in sick to work so he could stay with me.

⁓

And the dragon gave a huge bellow of pain. And he walked back into his cave. Then the Prince went and got his shield and walked over the mountain, avoiding the smoke and debris. The dragon snarled, and roared.

⁓

When I woke up the next day, Malachi wouldn't speak to me. I tried to jolly him through the first half of the morning, then let him avoid me until lunchtime.

"Hey, Ike. Can I make you a PB and J?"

"I'm not hungry."

"Oh, c'mon. I'll put more peanut butter on it. Way more. It'll be nice and messy."

He jutted his jaw forward and locked his eyes on the television, but as I started to walk away, he said, "Why don't you go lay down if you're so sick."

"Well, thanks for your concern, Dr. Snidely, but I'm feeling better today." Cringing at the cranky sound of that, I deliberately softened my tone and laid my hand on his head. "That was kind of rough yesterday, I know. But Dr. Ro said it's normal to be kind of rough the first few days after chemo, and then it gets better." He sat stone-faced. I knelt down beside him. "It gets better, right? Dr. Daddy gives me the shots and presto change-o—much better."

When he didn't answer, I stood and started to walk away.

"You're not sick," he suddenly burst out. "You're just lazy!"

"Malachi, I know you're upset about what happened yesterday, but I can't allow you to talk to me like that."

"You don't play—you don't read books—you just lay around on the couch all day!" His accusations started out halting and broken, escalating to a verbal tornado. "You don't want to go to the park or do art projects or science experiments like we always—"

"Malachi, I still want to do those things, but some days it's too hard for me."

"You don't even want to take care of us anymore! You don't even care!"

"You know that's not true."

"You're too lazy to do anything!"

"That's enough, Malachi!"

"You never do anything! Everybody does everything for you! You always get presents and mail. Nobody even *cares* about me!"

"Ike—"

"My teachers are always asking 'how's your *mom?*' and whenever you come to school, everybody's always saying 'what's wrong with your *mom?*' because you look *weird!* And you don't even care if you're embarrassing me!"

"Well, would you rather I didn't come at all?"

"Yes! 'Cuz you don't even wanna come anyway! You just wanna lay around."

"Ike," I searched around my head for some kind of appropriate response. "Life is full of stuff we have a tough time understanding. . . ."

"*Life is full of stuff we have a tough time understanding*," he mimicked me in a jeering falsetto.

"Hey!" I grabbed his arm and jerked him toward me. "I'm sorry this is hard for you, and someday you can tell your analyst how horrible it was having me for a mother, but in the meantime, I will not allow you to speak to me this way, do you understand?"

"I think you *like* having cancer! I wish *I* had cancer!"

God forgive me, I slapped him. Hard, and full across the face.

"Don't you ever, *ever* say that again," I gritted.

Malachi was too furious to do more than scream.

"You hit me!" he sobbed, stunned, indignant, wounded. "You *hit* me!"

My heart contorted, and I covered my guilty face with my hands.

"Get out of here," I said. "You go in your room and stay there."

He raced down the hall, kicking and swinging at all his inner dragons, knocking a picture off the wall and leaving angry gray scuff marks on the baseboard.

"I wish you would just die!" he cried before he slammed the door. "I hate you!"

But I hated myself more.

Choosy mothers, I mourned inside, choosy mothers choose Jif.

⁓

The prince looked round. And then, the dragon appeared. The prince lunged forward with his sword. He struck the dragon in the chest! The dragon bellowed and cried, it was as loud as thunder! Then the dragon fell to the ground and it breathed its last breath, and it was dead.

⁓

After five minutes, a glass of water, and a few deep breaths, I followed him down the hall.

"Ike?" I rapped gently. "Hey, Spike-man . . . can I come in?"

He didn't answer, but after a long moment, I heard him get up and unlock the door, and after another long moment, I opened it and stepped inside.

"All right. First, I'm sorry I hit you. That was wrong, wrong, *wrong*, and I'm sorry."

He sat at the end of his bed, fitting Legos together in their intricate, mysterious geometry, seeking to make sense of the scattered pieces.

"Malachi, I know you don't wish you had cancer. And I know you don't hate me. And I know that you know none of those other things you said are true. You're just mad because I'm sick, and that's—it's just . . ."

"It sucks," he said, daring me to challenge him on the borderline bad word.

"Yeah," I said, figuring he deserved a freebie. "It sucks."

"Mom," he looked up with brimming eyes and trembling chin. "I don't want you to—I don't wish—"

"I know. But I wouldn't blame you if you did. Because a few times lately . . . I've wished it myself. I've wished I would just die, Ike. There are times it seems like that would be easier."

He closed his eyes and shook his head, fighting not to cry.

"Mothers on TV are always dead."

It took me a moment to comprehend what he was saying, but considering it briefly, I realized he was right. Everybody from Bambi's mama to the first Mrs. Brady, *Pollyana*, *Chitty Chitty Bang Bang*, *Land Before Time*, *Cinderella*, *Snow White*—and the list goes on, from *The Courtship of Eddie's Father* to anything starring those lucrative little Olson twins. Perhaps it's the screenwriter's secret guilty wish. Maybe it's a tribute to the power of Mom to say that her death is the ultimate challenge any child character can face. Or maybe, it's just simpler than scripting the messy details of living. In any case, the dead mother theme seems to be one Hollywood has embraced with an Oedipal vengeance. I made a mental note never to take a role as the mother in a Disney movie. Talk about limited potential for character development.

"You're right," I had to laugh. "It always works out so nicely on TV, doesn't it? Everything turns out fine in thirty minutes minus commercials. But real life just keeps going. It gets messy. And it's a drag sometimes. Sometimes, you wish they'd just roll the credits and have it be over. But it just keeps on. No word from our sponsor. No nicely scripted denouement. You want to know what that means? *Denouement?*"

"No."

"Well, I'm telling you, anyway. It's a good word. It

means 'untying the knot.' It's the part of the show when everything gets untangled and works out fine." He tried to turn his face toward his pillow, but I pulled him onto my lap. "Malachi, I don't blame you for being mad at me. Everything's out of whack right now, and it seems like it's all my fault. But I really think I'm going to start getting better soon. And if I do die, it won't be because you wished it. Just the opposite. Every day I go on like this—well, it's hard, Ike. And I don't know if I would have had the courage to do it if it wasn't for you and Jerusha. You make me want to stay alive. You're so full of surprises. I just have to stay around and see how you turn out."

Then I laughed a little, because I was for some reason thinking about that old Kenny-you-big-buffoon incident.

⁓

When he got to the top of the mountain, he saw a patch of Magic-Moss! He took a medium-sized clump of moss, and started home. An hour later, he could see the Kingdom!

He hurried down the hill, through the trees and around the bushes. When he got home, he took some of the moss from his sack, wiped it on his mother's forehead and told his mother to eat just a little vine of it. When she did, he told her to get some rest and an hour later, he did the same thing. This made her better in a way, and sicker in another way. It healed her cancer, but it made her stay in bed a little longer each dose. And each time, he kept hugging her more and kissing her more.

And the queen said, "The moss is not the only thing that's healing me. Your love is too."

⁓

123

When I went to tuck Malachi in that night, I bent down to kiss his cheek, and he clung to my neck.

"Don't go yet."

"Okay."

"Will you rub my back?"

"Sure. Roll over."

I took up the hypnotic, rolling rhythm I've used on him from the time he was a baby, first his neck, then shoulders, ribcage, arms.

"Don't forget fingers and toes," he reminded me, and I squeezed each digit individually, working my thumbs across his palms.

"Mom?"

"Hmm?"

"I wish you still had long hair."

"How come?"

"You just looked more like your regular self with long hair."

"Well, it'll grow back. Think how often you need a haircut. Hair grows pretty fast."

"Yeah, but that'll be different hair. It won't be what you had before."

"C'mere," I said, pulling the blankets off him. "I'll show you a secret."

He followed me into my office, and I drew the paper bundle out of my desk, unrolling it to reveal my long braids neatly laid out within.

"Now, let me show you something else."

I dragged a chair to the closet and climbed up to a cardboard file box labeled IKE STUFF. It took me a few minutes to lay my hands on the baby book and then find inside it the envelope with his first golden curls.

"See? The hair you have now isn't the same, but it's great. Better, even. This was a baby's hair. And that's not who you are anymore. You're still Malachi, but you're big now. And smart. And brave."

"Isn't this who you are anymore?" he asked, fingering the auburn ropes.

"I don't know. But I'm still your mom. That part can't ever change." I pulled him onto my lap, knowing his protests were a mere formality. "It's just like the book where the mom always rocks her boy on her lap and tells him even when he's a grown-up man, 'I love you forever, I'll cherish you always, as long as I'm living my baby you'll be.'"

～

Two years later, the queen was much better. She felt a little dizzy now and then, but otherwise, she was pretty good. The prince was nine years old and the princess was seven years old. The king was forty-four and the queen was thirty-four. The queen was doing a lot more things than she had been doing in the past two years, she was playing with the kids, making them meals and spending some more time with the king, but everyone remembered the hardship that they had been through in the years before.

～

The braids in my desk drawer held a peculiar fascination for Malachi. He repeatedly asked to see them and spent hours arranging them according to length, by color variation, crisscrossed on the floor. He made them be snakes that bit and fought each other, but I did my best to ignore the mythological significance of that.

"Okay," I said one day. "Let's do an art project."

We took a hoop and covered it with a rabbit skin Jerusha had gotten at a trading post in Montana. Ike contributed found feathers, two arrowheads, and a rattle he'd made in Cub Scouts. Crystals came from teachers and friends. Agates from my mother. Last, I attached my braids to the bottom of the hoop, and then we hung the hoop on the wall. Looking at it, I remembered what Karen had said about the small things that connect us to our own life. What we'd made was not a funeral wreath. It was a circle of small things too important to be forgotten.

⌒

The years before had made them think how much they all were worth and how much pain it would be to lose each other. They made a mosaic on the castle wall. They put on a dragon's tooth (to show how powerful cancer was) a part of a giant crab shell (to represent the constellation cancer) and they told the town blacksmith to make a large metal heart and break it in half to represent the heartbroken times they'd been through in the past two years and put them on both sides of the mosaic. And to represent healing, some of the left-over dried magic moss that even if it was dried up, it would still refresh the house with a great smell and everyone remembered what they'd been through in their own way (even though it was like a code).

⌒

$\mathcal{Y}$ears later, I met Wendy Harpham when we were both slated to speak at the National Coalition for Cancer Survivorship conference in Albuquerque. Wendy is a physician, an author, and a survivor of non-

Hodgkin's lymphoma, and we found our common interests blossoming into friendship over the course of the weekend. She told me about the book she was working on, her third, entitled *When a Parent Has Cancer*, and when the book was released the following year, she sent me a copy. I pored over it, cringing at all the mistakes I'd made, congratulating myself on some of my better choices, and fervently wishing a similar resource had been available when I was first diagnosed. Tears burned my eyes as I read at the end of the final chapter the painfully accurate portrait she painted of my own family.

She spoke of trying to be an effective parent when "physical and emotional reserves are depleted." She talked about the uncertainty and the painful truths that must be told, about a child's grief and anger and fear. "Most painful of all, the parents with cancer suffer anxiety over possibly being unable to finish their most important lifework—raising their children. This anxiety breeds another," she continues, "a sense of urgency to do it right. Right now."

Though I couldn't see it at the time, Malachi's experience mirrored mine, emotion for emotion, challenge for challenge. He climbed his private mountain and came down changed, just as I did. Both of us discovered reservoirs of unexpected strength, but each of us left a little of our innocence behind.

"Savor the joyful moments and be nourished," are Wendy's wise words. "Meet the hard times and be fulfilled."

And then, Malachi finished his story, *like all fairy tales end, they all lived happily every after.*

8

Faith, Prayer, and Platitudes

> There lives more faith in honest doubt,
> Believe me, than in half the creeds.
>
> —ALFRED, LORD TENNYSON

*H*ear, oh people, the Gospel according to Billie Holiday, a woman who had the blues of Biblical proportion:

> *Why do I try to hold you near me?*
> *Why do I cry? You never hear me.*

When I hear that song, I don't think about a woman who's been ditched by her man, I think about Job. I think about how the Israelites cried out from the desert, and how Jesus cried out from the cross, "My God, my God, why have you forsaken me?" I think about the opening words of Psalm 10: "Why, O Lord, do you stand far off? Why do you hide yourself in times of trouble?" That's unrequited love on a cosmic level.

I'm invited now and then to speak about my cancer experience, and when people hear I'm a humorist, they expect a bunch of wacky, wacky anecdotes about wigs and vomit, so I tell them how I got through it all with my chin up and my spirits high.

Not!

I didn't find cancer all that funny, especially at the time.

Others who know I'm active in my church and used to be a United Methodist layspeaker expect me to tell how "Galoree Hal-lay-loo-yah! The laht of Jesus' mer-say shone down upon me an' I wuz hee-ulled!" And then, I guess I'm supposed to burst into a rousing chorus of "How Great Thou Art" so we can all join together in some kind of Tammy Faye mascara experience.

Also *not!*

I didn't find cancer all that inspiring, either.

Cancer didn't make me brave or noble or a woman of great faith. If anything, cancer showed me I wasn't nearly as brave or noble as I previously thought I was, and my faith turned out to be pretty much down there in the ol' mustard seed demographic.

This whole thing may very well have started January 1, 1994, when I made the world's stupidest New Year's resolution. I'd been flailing, struggling to figure out what I wanted to be when I grew up. I'd spent the last fifteen years making radio commercials, earnestly touting Moonlight Madness sales with Ca-raaaazy savings till midnight tonight! and saying things like "Quality products at low, low prices!" Or worse yet, things like "You've reached 1-900-FANTASY." Not much artistic or spiritual fulfillment there. So I resolved to say one prayer and one prayer only on behalf of my career for that entire year: "Lord, make me an instrument of Thy peace."

And I thought I meant it. But I quickly discovered this prayer was like asking Gary, "Say, honey, do these pants make me look fat?" In either case, there is vast potential for the wrong answer.

Now, Gary has learned over the years to field these trick questions. Apparently, God has not. Either that, or God simply doesn't fear my wrath to the extent that Gary does. Whatever—the opportunities that came to me were most definitely not the ones I'd had in mind.

With my initial cancer diagnosis, a great numbness descended. Now I know why Emily Dickinson called it the "Hour of Lead." I felt nothing, and I confess I did make stupid jokes about wigs and vomit. Of course I made jokes. Making jokes is what I do. I had to laugh. Because I couldn't cry. And I couldn't write and I couldn't sing and I could not pray.

My wonderful friend, the right Reverend Bob Holmes, was the pastor of our dear old St. Paul's United Methodist Church in Helena. He and his wife, Polly, are the truest, most generous people I know, and for a couple of old folks, they're amazingly hip. Bob called me on the phone, and I told him how much it frightened me when I couldn't find anything in my heart that felt like God, when I literally could not pray.

"That's okay," he said. "We'll pray for you."

And I know he did. And my family did, along with all our friends from Montana to New York City, and I wanted to have faith in the idea that this was going to somehow help me, but frankly, I was feeling pretty jaded on the subject. After all, Gary and I had prayed à la Gethsemene all the way to my biopsy surgery: "Please God! Don't let this be cancer!" Fat lot of good that did me. So, yeah, sure, Bob, crank up the ol' prayer chain. Meanwhile, pass me another radioactive cocktail. There's something I can put my faith in.

Of course, I didn't actually say that. It would be horrid to say anything like that to Bob or any of the other folks who were just trying to be loving and supportive, so I put on my

Brave Sick Person Face and said, "Thank you. That means so much to me."

Luckily, everyone with cancer is issued a Brave Sick Person Face. It comes with the wig. If your prognosis is really bad, you may even be upgraded to Saint Sick Person. It comes in handy, because the moment you're diagnosed with cancer, you become a platitude magnet. It's the truth. Cancer attracts proverbs like pocket lint on a LifeSaver. Pastel Precious Moments posters, plaques, and coffee mugs gather at your door like a gaggle of bug-eyed orphans. Aphorisms come flying from every direction.

People I hardly knew came up to me, saying stuff like, "The Lord never gives us more than we can bear" (although, in my experience, this seems to apply only to money and cleavage). Or "If you ask the Heavenly Father for bread, He will not give you a stone." (Perhaps the problem here is that God is thinking of the banana bread I bake, which could easily be mistaken for stone.) Or "You're an inspiration to us all." (I knew I must be looking really bad whenever somebody laid that one on me.) And then there's that lovely poem about footprints in the sand.

"So God tells him, 'The places where there's only one set of footprints—that's where I carried you,'" someone would tell me, blinking back tears, and I would struggle to resist adding, "Yeah, and that big ol' dent in the sand is where God dropped me on my freaking head!"

My personal favorite from The Big Book of Banality was (and feel free to sing along with me on this one) "That which does not kill us makes us stronger!" This is a little like saying that that which does not kill a seat cushion makes it a flotation device. But at least it gives us a Plan B to fall back on. After a while, I started getting this vision of searchlights, confetti, and the offstage announcer saying, "Congratulations!

You are the one millionth person to use that expression since Joni was diagnosed! What do we have for our winner, Don Pardo?"

Dr. Hagemeister, an oncologist at M. D. Anderson, once said to me, "Nobody wants to be a statistic, but everyone wants to know what their chances are." And so does everyone else. People asked me point-blank about my "prognosis." (translation: "So, are you gonna die?") And if I answered with the actual statistics, which were not overwhelmingly in my favor, there'd be a strained moment of silence, followed by "But you know, any one of us could be crossing the street tomorrow and get hit by a bus!" I know this was a genuine effort to make me feel better, to reassure me cancer wasn't really adding any element of uncertainty to my life. Or else bus-pedestrian accidents have risen to epidemic proportions. Maybe these people are just appallingly lax about looking both ways, but I'm pretty sure that until Stevie Wonder or Ray Charles gives up singing and starts driving a bus, cancer will still be significantly more perilous than crossing the street.

Free health advice was also abounding. There was a Shackley/Magic Herbal Tea/Bolivian Healing Kneesocks salesperson behind every tree, and every one of them had a full presentation to make on the Evils of Chemotherapy (or the Evils of Alternative Medicine or the Evils of Radiation or whatever didn't involve buying large quantities of their particular multilevel marketing product).

My sister Linda who sustained me with wonderful holistic medicines from her own garden and kitchen (many of which worked better than the pharmacy stuff) sent me a book called *Battle Cancer and Win!*, and I dove into it enthusiastically. It sounded so proactive in a butt-kicking, Schwartzenegger kind of way. But the book was a terrifying indictment of chemotherapy, and the battle plan basically consisted of a vegetable juice diet and frequent coffee enemas.

I guess maybe I could have dealt with the veggie juice, but hey—Mr. Coffee and I don't have that kind of relationship. I don't even know his first name! And how was I supposed to keep a straight face when the Starbucks girl asked me, "Have you tried the amaretto?" And how would that McDonald's lawsuit have sounded with the testimony beginning, "Well, I went to swish this coffee up my ass, and I had no idea it was going to be so hot!"

Of course, the worst side effect was pointed out in an interview with Dr. Robert Buckman, whom I like to call "the Monty Python of Cancer Research." When a reporter asked him about the possible dangers of coffee enema therapy, he commented off the cuff, "Well, I should think it would seriously affect the taste of the coffee!"

My ultimate response to the cancer battle plan: "Retreat!"

Still, as the months wore on and my jaded exterior wore down, I was hungry for hope, craving for comfort. One day on television, I saw a little entertainment news blurb about the man who, as a boy, had played Peter Brady on *The Brady Bunch* and had recently been diagnosed with cancer. His TV siblings praised him for his positive attitude, and he boldly told the interviewer, "I got cancer, but cancer didn't get me!"

I welled up and clutched the remote control to my heart. The first thing that came to my mind was, "I want to be like that. I want to be able to stand there with my dignity and my sense of humor intact and say cancer hasn't gotten me." The second thing that came to my mind was, "Peter Brady is now my spiritual guru? How pathetic is that?!"

I was rescued from this deluge of chicken soup for the soul by two women I regard as life rafts in the storm-tossed sea of this whole experience: Melodie King and Tess Walker.

Melodie's daughters had baby-sat for us in Pennsylvania, and her husband was transferred to Houston at the same time Gary was. I resisted when Melodie invited us all to Thanksgiving dinner at her home the weekend I was diagnosed. We didn't really know each other very well, and I felt guilty about the fact that, while she was undergoing chemo the previous year, my entire communication with her had consisted of an occasional uncomfortable "Tell your mom if there's anything I can do . . . "

The day turned out to be an oasis. Just to see Melodie sitting there, alive, with hair, being happy and almost healthy again, was encouraging. She spoke candidly about indelicate aspects of treatment that had somehow slipped my oncologist's mind (or maybe she just didn't want to scare me). I left feeling ready to go forward.

"Melodie," I said as we did that thing where you say you're leaving, then stand in the driveway talking for another twenty minutes, "I feel like such a heel. You've been so great to me this week, and I was absolutely no help at all when you were going through it."

"But there was nothing you could have done," she told me. "The only person who can help is someone who's been there. Someone who'd been there helped me. And now I'm helping you. And someday, you'll help someone else, and that's how you'll know you got through it, too."

Tess was the friend of a realtor who was hoping to sell us a house before I was diagnosed. She'd been through chemo for both lymphoma and leukemia and is now active in CanCare, an interfaith ministry that trains cancer survivors to offer one-to-one support to the newly diagnosed. She called me several times throughout my treatment, providing valuable information and the emotional support that can truly only come from someone who's been there, done that.

"You know what I like about you, Tess?" I said to her one day. "You get the chemo jokes. And you've never once told me that which does not kill me makes me stronger."

"Mmm," she said, "you'll get a lot of that. Just understand that it's truly a loving impulse that guides the majority of people."

"Even the ones who feel compelled to share the gory, graphic description of how Great-Aunt Tillie came down with this very same kind of cancer and died an agonizing, lingering death?"

"But she was a real trooper to the end, by golly!" Tess laughed, having heard the same story a thousand times. "Yes. I think they're just trying to find some way to connect. I mean, look at it from their side—what are they allowed to say? Seriously. What can they say that would make it any easier? Nothing. But if they say nothing, they're being cold and insensitive. Damned if they do, damned if they don't."

"Yeah, I guess you're right. I hadn't thought of it that way."

"I always tell people not to say 'if there's anything I can do . . .,' because, you know, the sick person isn't going to ask them to do anything ninety-nine times out of a hundred. I tell them, 'If you really mean it, make a specific offer.'"

"Like my sister hiring someone to clean my house."

"Exactly. Bring supper over—but in a disposable container I don't have to wash and return. Pick my kids up from school or take them to the movies. Mow the lawn. Weed the flowerbed. Or just say, 'I'm sorry this is happening to you. I care.'"

"And then let the conversation move on to something other than cancer."

"Right!" Tess laughed. "Anyway . . . just remember their hearts are aching, too. You don't understand what they're going through any more than they understand what it is for you. Though I know it gets weary," she sighed, "comforting all those people who call to comfort you."

"Still," I said, "it's a small price to pay for all that free casserole."

*P*erhaps my inability to pray for myself during those first few months of chemo stemmed from my early relationship with God having been based primarily on fear. (I suspect the same goes for many of my fellow dirge-dogging, Thee-Thou-ing guilt-ridden products of parochial school.) From the time I was a tyke in a succession of fundamentalist religious schools (Mom and Dad were afraid public school would be a bad influence), I was indoctrinated with the synodical party line. *The Lord thy God is a jealous God*, a theososaurus who sat in heaven bitch-slapping the unbaptized and smoking Sodomites like cheap cigars. I had a child's complete faith in this God and in the notion that he could, would, and probably should destroy me should I fail in the total renunciation of "the devil, the world, and my sinful flesh."

Growing up in the Wisconsin Evangelical Lutheran Synod, I was told the planet Earth is, according to the Usher Time Line, six thousand years old. This sounded ancient in the extreme to my child mind, so I had no cause to disbelieve it. But when I began to study the natural sciences, I realized that six thousand years is less than the shelf life of a Hostess Twinkie, that there are Raisinets under your sofa cushion older than that.

I was told all Jews go to hell. Do not pass go, do not collect two hundred dollars. They rejected Jesus, they killed the Messiah—they're toast. But when I taught creative drama classes at a Jewish day school, I observed a loving community, committed to their children and their faith. If the God at work in my life was a God who could turn a deaf ear toward these people (not to mention the children of Auschwitz) I was in deep, deep trouble.

I was told that the Bible clearly states women are not to become ministers, teach men, or have any voice or vote in church other than through that of their husband. But looking around the churches in which I grew up, I saw the women doing the lion's share of the work.

As I struggled through four years of Lutheran high school, vague suspicions and doubts began to plague me. Maybe carbon dating was not the tool of Satan and his band of atheist scientists after all. Maybe a pastor who grew up in Germany in the 1940s has some not-so-kosher feelings about Jews. Maybe men of bygone eras had political reasons for silencing women. As these and other niggling cracks appeared in the foundation of my belief system, I felt less and less worthy of God's mercy.

But it was that stinkin' rotten Satan creating all my doubts, I kept telling myself. It was my own fault for having such a crappy little weak-chinned faith. I was determined to cling to the dogma I'd been raised with, until one crisp October night when I got into a heavy conversation with that slightly geeky, sweetly bookish boy I met in college.

He looked like a young Franz Kafka. He had an English major's vocabulary and a nineteen-year-old farm boy's healthy interest in flesh, sinful and otherwise. Never in my life had I smoked a cigarette, tasted alcohol, or met anyone like him.

"Joni, you're one of the smartest, most opinionated people I know," he said, propping his elbows on a corner table at Wunder Bar, an establishment directly adjacent to campus where English and theater majors congregated to drink beer and get pedantic. "But it's like you're afraid to think for yourself on this subject. Like you think you're going to go to your eternal damnation if you so much as question what people have been telling you."

"As opposed to having original thoughts like 'God is dead' and 'Religion is the opiate of the masses'?"

"You forgot 'Organized religion is evil,'" he laughed good-naturedly.

"See, you're just as entrenched in the beliefs you were brought up with," I told him primly. "Only difference is—you were brought up by hippies."

"Hey, hippies were a lot more in tune with the whole Jesus message than most church types. He was all about love, man. He was all about love thy neighbor. But that message has been totally perverted by centuries of political agenda. It's like Tolstoy said, 'The only problem with Christianity is that no one has ever tried it.'"

"You can't just take the passages you like and throw out the rest because it doesn't suit your agenda," I flatly stated.

"But that's exactly what's been done!" argued the young Kafka. "The Bible is like a salad bar from which the magnates of organized religion pick and choose whatever meaning best serves their political agenda. What about the Apocrypha? And all that other stuff they left out?"

"That stuff isn't the *Bible*. The Bible is the only true and inspired word of God, and John says at the very end of Revelations not to add or subtract anything. It warns us 'not to change a jot nor tiddle.'"

"John was talking about Revelations itself, Joni. He knew people would try to change it because it makes him come off like a freaking lunatic. He was probably totally stoned when he wrote it. You can't apply that admonition to the Bible, because the Bible didn't exist until hundreds of years later."

"Oh, geez ⌐⌐ that's right." A chink appeared in my apostolic armor, and I felt my blessed assurance slipping more than a tiddle. Suddenly, I wasn't sure what I actually believed and what I was automatically regurgitating from confirmation class. "You're right. The Bible as we know it was assembled at the Council of Nicea in A.D. 325."

"Wow!" Pseudo-Franz looked at me across the table, his expression warm with Heineken and affection. "I can't believe you actually know that."

A great sadness—and an even greater guilt—swept over me. I knew I could no longer struggle to defend ideas about which I had lots of knowledge but in which I had no real faith. I'd tried my best to justify these misogynist, anti-Semitic doctrines to other people, even as I grew more and more uncomfortable with them myself. But as my editor said to me just the other day, "You can't go against your gut."

When the barkeep sounded the last call for alcohol, it was as if a pendulum swung inside me. With one grand *what the hell*, I threw the baby Jesus out with the holy bath water, ordered up a double shot of Jack Daniel's, and lost my virginity not four hours later.

*F*or years, I tried not to think about religion in general, but I wanted to give my children the good things a church environment has to offer, so after they were born, we came and went for a while, practicing a religion that was roughly 70 percent social, 20 percent spiritual, and 10 percent force of habit. We prayed with our children at bedtime, said grace with them at the supper table, and told them that when you pray for someone, an angel comes to sit on their shoulder. I prayed silently when I was afraid or frustrated. And then there was that incredibly stupid New Year's resolution.

All in all, I thought I was a fair-to-middlin' Christian until cancer came and started whispering in my ear. It was easy to imagine I was being punished or, worse yet, ignored by a God who was fed up with my mediocre allegiance and poor piety performance stats. I hadn't been to services in four years—not since we left our *fun* church in Montana for the outer darkness of the East Coast, where they all dressed up too much. I cussed like a sailor and, given the choice, would have gladly eaten stained glass rather than watch *The 700 Club*. Not exactly God's A-list material by most people's standards.

So I redoubled my efforts to study the Bible, scoured the text for every story of physical healing, searching specifically for the common ingredients that formed the miraculous recipe, straining to figure out what those people did that I was incapable of. Why did Jesus have to go around being so dang hyperbolic about everything, I wondered. I wanted some specific, step-by-step instructions, dammit, and all I was getting was mustard seeds and vineyards and beatitudes out the wazoo. Instead of being comforted or inspired by the miracles Jesus performed, I felt dark surges of anger and jealousy. That lousy blind man probably went back to panhandling the next day. And Jairus's daughter—what did that little snot ever do to deserve a second chance? The deeper I waded, the more disillusioned I became. It frightened me to read about people who'd "hardened their hearts" because that's exactly how I felt.

Hardened. Stony.

The living, dynamic, and loving God was obscured by the angry, judging, stolid one in the Renaissance paintings;

the one who was dark and foreboding and distinctly male. That was a God I was afraid to know, and so I drifted farther and farther away from the real thing. I never had any doubt about the existence of God, only his abiding interest in a puny, faithless Moabite like me.

*B*ecause of the depletion of the immune system during chemo, it's imperative that the long-line and cath port be kept as dry and sterile as possible. If the site became infected, the line had to be replaced via a not very nice procedure that I had no desire to repeat, so I took every precaution, including showering with my arm bound up in a plastic bread bag, sticking outside the curtain.

Even so, the shower is such a liberating place, isn't it? You're buck naked. You're singing the *Love Boat* theme song like you're channeling Ethel Merman or something. Whatever motions and masquerades we go through in the outer world, there are no pretenses to be upheld in the shower.

So maybe that's why after months of this glib-talking, nonfeeling, zombie autopilot thing I'd been on, I was standing in the shower one day, and I started to weep.

"Mama," I heard myself sobbing, "Mama . . . mama . . . I can't take this anymore. . . ." I begged for strength, for forgiveness, for the preservation of my life, and for any, any, any kind of relief, up to and including death.

What echoed off the tile walls, I suddenly realized, was *praying*. And when I realized I was praying—*finally* praying—*really* praying—I got pissed. I felt like after six months on hold, I finally had me a customer service representative on the line, and I was going to let 'er have it.

"I never once asked you *why me,* but why my family? My parents did not deserve to be put through this. My children did not deserve to witness this. My husband did not deserve to share in this. *Instrument of your peace?* What a bunch of crap! You've made me a source of pain to everyone I care about! Are you even paying *attention* here? Do you see *what's going on?"* I sobbed, rocking on the ledge of the tub, not caring that water was streaming through the plastic bag on my arm and onto the floor. "I asked you for bread, and you gave me a big fat fucking *stone.*"

I wish I could report some blinding epiphany here, but there was no thunderclap, no burning bush.

Later, though, when I'd wiped up the floor and was sitting there in my bathrobe, it occurred to me that you don't get that angry at someone who isn't there. You don't stand there cussing out someone who's far off. And at that moment, God didn't feel far off.

I didn't particularly like God, but God was not far off.

And in the days that followed, I began to feel a few soft spots in the hardness of my heart. I'd never addressed God in the feminine before. If anyone had asked me, I would have said that the being of God defies boundaries of gender and other human limitations, but I'd still say "Our Father" just in case Michelangelo's paternal Almighty was actually standing there, waiting to strike me dead. At this moment, however, the comfort I was seeking was richly feminine in character, and I felt heard by a richly maternal power.

I thought about all the prayers I'd prayed so fervently over the years. "Send me, show me, give me the opportunity, create in me a clean heart, oh God," and of course (the biggie!) "Thy will be done." Truth be told, I never wanted those prayers answered. I wanted my agenda followed. I wanted my career as an actress, and God was supposed to be the booking agent, not the artistic director. I tried to suck up by saying thanks for everything first, of course, tried to strike deals and plea bargains by saying what I was supposed to say. But when I prayed, "Lord make me an instrument of thy peace," I conveniently forgot one small detail: before it can be played by a master, an instrument has to be stretched and twisted and cranked into tune.

Geez, I hate that.

After all, mine was such a noble prayer, such a lofty ambition! What did Mother Teresa have that I didn't besides a big nose and a state funeral? But a God to whom we recite words like "Thy will" and "Thy peace"—this is a God who seems to stand very far off indeed.

In reality, of course, it's us. We're the ones keeping our distance. We don't say to our neighbor, "Thy dog poopeth in my yard." We don't go up to our boss and plead, "Give us this payday our daily bread." Yet, for some reason, this is the distance with which we're taught to pray. And such a comfortable distance it is. Not having God looking over our shoulder makes filing our taxes so much less complicated, not to mention disciplining our children or driving on by that guy with the HUNGRY VIETNAM VET sign. We look so much better from this distance, we don't cross it until we absolutely have to.

We'd rather do a weekly drive-thru worship at the local Christ-in-a-Box—if we even do that. Lip service and political correctness are marketed as viable substitutes for spirituality and commitment. When we can't confine God in a framework of human characteristics, we shroud God in mystery, because the idea of God actually being accessible to us, well, that would mean we are accessible to God. And that's a terrifying concept.

I believe faith is the essence, a simple solution, yet too hard for most people to practice," Dr. Bernie Siegel says in *Love, Medicine, and Miracles.*

Dr. Ro once said to me, "Believing that you are going to live may not guarantee that you are going to live, but believing that you are going to die will most certainly reduce your chances of survival."

Dr. Paul Donaldson, the family practitioner who delivered both my children, said more succinctly, "If it works, I believe in it."

My sister Janis speaks of "the cone of power," a sort of karmic umbrella we four sisters raise when one of us is in crisis. When I was diagnosed, I was in Houston, Janis was in San Jose, Linda was in Montana, and Diana had just moved to Melbourne, Australia. My inner vision of that cone of power, beaming upward from this wide circle to a single point of energy, sustained me through more than one long night.

The comfort I prayed for when I cried out to the Mama God came to me in the person of (who else?) Mom when she flew down from Montana, took care of the kids, took care of me, and gave Gary some relief. When my mother was with me and sometimes when she wasn't, I swear I could physically feel her powerful prayers surrounding me. I envisioned them as a field of unfiltered light as I lay listening to the same Chet Atkins and Hank Snow music she played for me when I was a child with chicken pox.

Reverend Bob sent me a series of tapes to which I listened while I was receiving treatments. On them, he played his fiddle and guitar, sang songs we'd sung together in church years earlier, and talked to me in a voice that is the aural equivalent of warm wheat bread with honey. He included selections by the St. Paul's choir and Montana Logging and Ballet Company, blending the voices of friends, rich harmony, and good humor. I realized, as I began to rely more and more on these visualizations that Bob was right; I was able to stop trying so hard to pray, because they were praying for me. My own faith started out fragile and crumbled like a rice cake the minute the shit hit the fan, but theirs stood, an unshakable fortress around me.

I attribute my remission, at least in part, to the way the people who loved me lifted me up before God, and in answer to any hairy-eyeballed skeptic, I would point to studies that have proved the power of prayer. It stands to reason that good vibes decrease free radicals and bad vibes increase them. Anyone who's ever felt heated anger or cold fear would have to acknowledge that the effects of stress, depression, and hatred reach beyond the psychological universe into the physical one, as do the powerful tonics of love, joy, and forgiveness.

There was a Creator loving enough to sacrifice a son, a Spirit strong enough to encompass all people, a Christ compassionate enough to let them pound nails through his hands. Consider the brutal reality of that for a moment, and the distant, unforgiving God persona simply makes no sense. And as far as my ability (or lack of it) to earn God's love and favor, I finally happened on a Bible passage that told me what I needed to know.

"This is my commandment: that you love one another as I have loved you," Jesus tells his disciples in the Book of John. "No one has greater love than this, to lay down his life for his friends. You are my friends, if you do as I command you. I do not call you servants any longer."

$y$our turning point," Silverberg once said to me, "will come when you're able to turn this experience into something positive. You'll feel empowered again—less like a victim—if you find a way to help someone else." And he was right.

In the years since chemo, the opportunities I prayed for when I lined out my schedule to the booking-agent God have come from a variety of surprising directions. I was asked to speak at an AIDS benefit and discovered I had something meaningful to say. I joined Anderson Network, through which someone who's just been diagnosed with cancer is put in touch with someone who's been there, and volunteered to help out at M. D. Anderson's survivorship conferences. I made myself available through the school guidance counselor to other moms who are going through chemo and need help with baby-sitting, driving, shopping, resources, or just need the proverbial shoulder.

Grateful as I was to have others reach out to me when I was hurting, I've found even more comfort in being on the giving end of the same kindnesses that were extended to me. Having matured a little, mellowed a lot, I discover I'm better prepared for an abundance of wonderful things that come into my life (including the fact that you're holding this book in your hands right now!) Things I never even knew I was praying for and might not have otherwise recognized as blessings.

It's kind of like Jerusha's first waffle.

"Trust me," I kept telling her, "it's just like bread, only better!"

She finally took a small bite.

"Hmmm . . . ridgey," she said. "You wouldn't really

want to put peanut butter on it. . . ." She took another bite. "But I like it!"

"See?" I credoed. "Sometimes, you gotta have faith."

January 1, 1995. My only New Year's resolution was to remain alive until 1996, and each year since then, I've made the same commitment, as I close another calendar book filled with joys and opportunities (along with oncology appointments and CAT scans). Filled with hope, I look forward to each coming year. And I pray, asking for bread, but emotionally and spiritually prepared to receive . . . a waffle.

"*T*here are three kinds of lies," Mark Twain once said. "Lies, damned lies, and statistics." Another wise man, my own Gar Bear, once said to me, "Who cares about those numbers? You're either a hunded percent alive or you're dead, and frankly, the kids and I don't give a flying neon lizard shit what seven out of ten other people are doing."

The insurance company, on the other hand, can't function without plugging me into their Ouija Board of tables and spreadsheets. They crack out their little calculators and figure up my blah-blah percent chance of survival, placing bets on whether I'm going to live the optimistic "five years or more" and placing their faith in the flow charts and graph lines.

They're in for a rude surprise. I plan to be an aggressive health-care consumer for a long time to come. They're going to have to keep shelling out for those CAT scans and follow-up visits and even a couple more rounds of chemo, if that's what it takes, as I plan to wedge God for every single day I can get.

I refer to myself as a cancer survivor as opposed to a cancer victim. I chant the words *survival and healing* in one of my meditations. Survival and healing are certainly two things I strive for. However, I reject the narrow definition of those words. If cancer sucks all the joy out of your life, you have not survived it. If cancer is a threshold you cross to leave physical life and become part of a greater life, which may not be physical but is just as real as radio waves, you are healed.

Something that really bugs me—and I mean even worse than God screwing up my order—is when people try to tell someone with cancer if their faith is strong enough, they'll be healed. The obvious implication here is that, if they're not healed (in the narrowest sense of the word), their faith was somehow lacking. There's an assumption that if God doesn't answer our prayer as mandated, he must be screening calls from those of us who lack the spiritual ta-tas to get his attention. There's little room for the idea that healing and death often come hand in hand. There's little respect for the journey that takes us beyond the polyester realm of flesh, bones, Wal-Mart, and the Weather Channel. We're so absorbed in our quest for physical things, we forget that survival is a given. It just doesn't necessarily come in a human-shaped container.

When I look at it from a purely selfish point of view, it's a win-win situation for me. Either I get to stay on this fantastically entertaining planet, or I get to meet Jesus and throw my arms around him and finally get a few straight answers, for a change! It's the blessed assurance that he's there that makes me want more than ever to raise my family and do my work and love my neighbor and cherish the heck out of this oh-most-bodacious of birthday gifts—*life!*

"So and so died, on such and such a day," the obituaries

often read, "having lost her battle with cancer." As if death was the triumph of cancer and the defeat of her soul. But wouldn't it be a loss if someone—anyone—had a chance to grow in spirit and chose not to? What a crushing defeat if a person lived for fifty years after a cancer diagnosis, but chose to be embittered rather than enlightened by the experience.

These days, I have occasion to meet and speak with a great many people who have cancer or AIDS (or both.) I've seen several of them die, but I have not witnessed one of them lose. They've shown me that part of us that lingers after we leave.

It's nothing we've done.

It's everything we've given.

There is an undeniably real force that flows from beyond our understanding, flows through us into others and through others into us. Even when our faith stumbles and our prayers run out, when our strength fails and there are no words, it flows.

Ubi caritas et amour, ubi caritas Deus ib.

Where love and caring are, there is God.

The comfort, the energy, the laughter, and love—if that isn't sacred grace, I don't know what is. We don't have to *do* it; it's what we're made of. That part of us *is* part of God. That part of us will always survive.

I know it as surely as I know my friend.

9

What's a Nice Girl Like Me. . .

Fair seed-time had my soul, and I grew up
Fostered alike by beauty and by fear.

—WILLIAM WORDSWORTH

I'm a nice girl. A bright girl. A God-fearing, bookish sensible-shoe kind of girl. My wild oats gave way to Quaker Oats by the time I was twenty-one. Even before that, a sturdy Lutheran upbringing instilled enough guilt to prevent me from doing anything really kinky. Now, I've been married to the same wonderful old grizzly bear seemingly forever, and if our sex was any safer, we'd have to wear crossing-guard uniforms. I'm always there on PTO volunteer day. I pay my power and phone bills regularly. I don't do drugs. I don't do biker bars or gay bars. I don't even do *candy* bars.

What could AIDS have to do with a nice girl like me?

Before Gary and I moved to northern California in the early eighties, I'd never even heard of AIDS. While we were there, though, we listened to Bay Area radio stations. Bizarre late-night talk shows were filled with crackpots claiming that illegal aliens from Haiti were infected with a terrible disease, that gay men in the bathhouses were spreading it, that public toilets were no longer safe to use, that the blood supply was tainted, that it could be carried by mosquitoes, that health workers were threatening to strike for fear of the inadequate precautions being taken to protect them, that this was God's punishment raining down upon all those who lived depraved and promiscuous lifestyles.

When I saw in the *San Francisco Chronicle* that Rock Hudson had died of the disease, I said to Gary, "Oh my, do you think he was gay?"

"No, honey," Gary said, "he was a closet Haitian."

"But Rock Hudson? Did he look gay to you?"

"Does anybody?"

"Well, sure. Some guys do."

"Well," Gary said, "those guys are in trouble. We're looking at the leprosy of the modern age. People are starting to freak out because they don't know what it is. They just know it's something scary, and they want someone to hang it on. And it's not like our society ever needed much of an excuse for gay-bashing in the first place."

By the time the rumors of the early eighties blossomed into the designer cause of the early nineties, information was a lot less sketchy and a lot more terrifying, and public apprehension expanded to include hemophiliacs and anyone who could hum more than one number from the score of *Cats*. Gary and I shook our heads sadly over stories of a house being burned down because the neighbors feared the little HIV-positive boys who lived there; of a gay man being fired from his job when employers became convinced a bout with the flu was actually the onset of AIDS; of emergency medical treatment being denied an accident victim who somehow seemed gay to the ambulance attendant.

Later, when we were living in the Philly area, I read about the AIDS-infected infants and toddlers in New York who were dumped into a system of foster care unable to find anyone willing to touch them, until they were taken in by one brave woman called Mother Hale. Needless to say, she soon had a very large family, and since the death of this great lady, her work has been carried on by her daughter Dr. Lorraine Hale. I wanted to help—being so nice and all—so I started sending twenty dollars a month to Hale House. Of course, I never actually went to Hale House, even though I lived sixty minutes from New York City for four years. I just sent my twenty bucks whenever I could afford it. That was as close as I wanted to get. Like many people who missed the sixties but kinda like the music, I enjoyed thinking of myself as "involved," and hey—babies are innocent; it couldn't be their fault they have AIDS. This felt like a warm, fuzzy charity upon which I could congratulate myself.

Then Howard Ashman died of AIDS. Remember Howard Ashman? The songwriter "who gave the Little Mermaid her voice" and made a Broadway star out of a man-eating plant in *Little Shop of Horrors*? He earned a posthumous Oscar for his work on Disney's *Beauty and the Beast*. His death was a great loss to American musical theater, and here again — we're talking Disney, for pete's sake. How much of a pervert could he have been?

So here again, I felt oh so socially conscious when I was asked to teach a theater workshop and chose for my theme *Beauty and the Beast: AIDS in the American Theater*. I worked with David, an old acquaintance, a director, actor, and dad. We talked to our students about Ashman, *Angels in America*, *Falsettos*, and how the epidemic had affected the arts in general.

After class, we went for coffee, discussing how we could

develop the concept further for other venues. David was directing a play called *Touch Me* and hoped to get a touring company together. We hugged and parted with promises to stay in touch, but when I called several months later, David was dead.

*T*he following year, Gary and I sat in the library, staring at a heavy reference tome.

Under non-Hodgkin's lymphoma, terrifying phrases emerged from the blur of medical terminology.

. . . cancer of the lymphatic system . . .

. . . non-favorable prognosis . . .

. . . often a complication of AIDS . . .

Now here's something you never expect to hear yourself praying: "God, please let me have just cancer!"

I'd been tested a few years earlier, but they tested me again. And again. Negative. Gary and I breathed a mutual and deep sigh of relief. As serious as my situation was, I could still claim my place in a nice, straight clean-living HIV-negative world. I wasn't one of those HIV-positive people who were . . . well, wherever they were, doing . . . whatever it is they do.

Where many of them were, I soon discovered, was exactly where I was: at the chemotherapy clinic. And they were doing the same thing I was doing: hoping despite statistics, laughing despite pain, rolling up their sleeve again, and watching the O.J. trial from an IV ward recliner. They had jobs and lives, faces and names. They had children.

We sat in a long row of naugahyde chairs, tethered to our IV trees, comparing HMO horror stories, sharing information and resources, talking about traffic, protein supplements, dreams for the future. We traded tapes for our Sony

Walkmans—alpha waves, Dr. Bernie Seigel, 50 Great Moments in Opera—respecting one another's need to retreat now and then, each into the privacy of our own headphones. When we were few (room B held only two or three), we sometimes spoke more intimately of feeling betrayed by our bodies and abandoned by our antibodies, of missing our lovers, of being afraid to use the chained pen at the bank because it had other people's germs on it or not daring to turn down the grocery store aisle if we heard someone cough. We discussed baldness, vomiting, mouth sores, constipation that binds you up like a bale of hay, diarrhea that turns you inside out, toenails that fall off while you're in the bathtub, and a variety of other topics any sane person would rather not be involved in.

It wasn't so much to commiserate as to build a frame of reference, to chart some sort of cartography through this unfamiliar land. Each of our journeys was unique, but we all came to this common place, this painfully sterile room with its piercing-white linoleum. It seemed less dangerous somehow, knowing the ungentle place was inhabited by gentle people.

*A*nother book sent to me by my sister Linda recommended Tai Chi as a healing activity, so I enrolled in a class, hoping it would put me in touch with my chi—that part of me that is my "vital energy."

At first, the mystic music and moony instructor put me more in touch with that part of me that giggles uncontrollably, but I was soon swept into the graceful uniformity, the hypnotic ranks and rows of gliding hands and whispering feet. Synchronized in a flow of homogeneous motion, focused on breathing, healing, remaining on the planet.

After five or six consecutive Tuesday evenings, my chi

was a-flowin', baby. My chi was expanding and descending. I was filled with chi. I was a chia pet.

Moving, swimming in my private dusk, I forgot the fluorescent lights gleaming off my naked head and floated above the portable IV pump that chirped periodically as if to announce, "Adriamycin! It's not just for breakfast any more!"

During a five-minute break, I went to get a drink from the water fountain, and when I stood up, the young man in line behind me turned toward the fountain and inhaled sharply, visibly startled by my appearance. He stood there for a moment, looking at me, and then he crossed to the other side of the gym and got in line to drink from the other water fountain.

Before I could cry after him, "Wait! You don't understand! I'm *nice!*" the lights dimmed, the soft, spacey music started up again, and we all took our places to continue.

But try as I might, I couldn't seem to align myself with the orderly ranks and rows any longer. I wasn't angry, exactly. But I suddenly felt balder and sicker than I had a moment earlier, devitalized somehow, depleted. I saw myself caught up in an epidemic that has less to do with the mutating of cells or the spreading of a virus than it has to do with the seeping of ignorance and the contagion of fear, an eagerness to condemn, a reluctance to empathize. Perhaps, the most painful thing about it was knowing that six months earlier, I was a carrier of that plague. I had spoken with the political correctness of an invincible post-baby-boom land-of-plenty ethicist, but when it came to putting my mouth to that fountain, I might have done the same thing he did. I would have been just as afraid. Just as revolted.

There's a very human need to say, "I am separate from that. Thank God, that could never happen to me. Thank God, I'm safe." With razor-sharp instincts for self-preservation, we convince ourselves that our choices are blessed, our lifestyle ordained. Anyone not blessed and ordained as we— well, they deserve what they get. They must deserve it, or where is God?

When we look at the man in the hands of hospice care, the young mother entangled in the spider's web of welfare, or the PLEASE HELP sign carrier standing on the boulevard, we need to stamp a label on their forehead. FREELOADER. JUNKIE. PROMISCUOUS. FAG. Even when we look at the children, the kindest thing we will allow is VICTIM. It's too hard to say, "There but for the grace of God go I." Most of us are unwilling to see a connection between ourselves or our children and a world we perceive as bereft of hope. It's too difficult to see, through the obscuring cloud of frightening statistics and inflated insurance company claims about the cost of AIDS care and research, that the advances being made through that research will expand our understanding of everything from hepatitis to the common cold, and more important, that caring for others enriches us as individuals and enhances us as a civilization. The ability to give that care will ultimately heal us all.

At this writing, researchers are agonizingly close to a cure for non-Hodgkin's lymphoma, developed in no small part through funding for AIDS research, clinical trials that led to the approval of new techniques, drastically reducing the NHL mortality rate over the last five years and quite possibly enabling me to see my children grow up. Men and women—many with AIDS—stepped forward for those clinical trials, saying, "Hit me, Doc. I know I'm probably not going to live, but I'm going to try, and what you learn might give someone else a chance."

And that someone else was me. The nice girl. The straight girl. Safe and separate in my HIV-negative world.

10

Slow Dance with a Good Man

There are three things which are too wonderful for me;
yea, four things which I know not:
the way of an eagle in the air,
the way of a serpent on a rock,
the way of a ship upon the sea,
and the way of a man with a maid.

—PROVERBS 30:18-19

*T*hey say a good man is hard to find. But a *really* good man is hard to lose.

The first time I saw Gary Rodgers, he was riding a bicycle through a blizzard. I was sitting in a window booth at the Bacchus Pub in Bozeman, Montana, with three other actors from the theater company with which I was touring, and I still recall my exact words.

"What kind of moron rides a bicycle through a blizzard?"

"Oh, I know him," said Gwen, one of my onstage compadres. "You two would be great together. He's really strange, too."

"Gee, thanks," I said, watching through the window as he skimmed up onto the sidewalk.

"He lives out in the toolies like a hermit or something.

And he takes one or two classes at MSU every semester just so he can do theater and use the gym. He must have like fifty different degrees by now."

She turned away to discuss her drink order with the waiter, but I couldn't stop watching out the window. The frosty rider dismounted and kicked free a slotted space in the iced-over bike rack. Standing by a streetlight that still sported an enormous Santa Claus, he pulled off his watch cap and wiped it across his forehead, then pulled a chain from his pocket and started fiddling with a combination lock.

He was wearing a brown-and-white Alpine sweater and sage-colored wool pants tucked into dark green gaiters. White frost clung to his eyebrows and to an anachronistic handlebar mustache that almost met his equally outmoded muttonchop sideburns, emphasizing his prominent nose and square jaw. The overall effect was sort of an army-navy-surplus-barbershop-singer-of-the-Yukon look. He locked the bike to the metal frame and tucked his ponytail inside the watch cap, resettling it at an angle that was more haphazard than jaunty.

My breath had created a soft gray fog on the glass, and I wiped my hand across it so I could watch him as he crossed at the corner and disappeared down the dark street that swirled and shadowed and took him in, as if he'd walked off into a snow globe.

Later that evening, Gwen and I went to see some friends of hers in a university production of *Fiddler on the Roof*, and afterward, to a backstage gathering of theater people, musicians, and other far-out and groovy types who tend to be overeducated and undermotivated. Standing there, I overheard two men lamenting the lack of true theatrical art in this commercial sea of musical comedy shtick crap currently being done, and since I was making a living doing shtick crap with a touring musical comedy troupe at the time, I figured I had the authority to march over and set them straight.

"Excuse me," I began my five-minute diatribe, "but anyone who doesn't think comedy is an artform certainly hasn't read much Shakespeare, have they?" I went on to cover everything from the French neo-classics to Jerry Lewis in *The Nutty Professor.*

When I finally paused to inhale, one of the men stepped forward, enveloped me in his arms, and whispered, "I love you."

Of course, I didn't believe him. And to this day, I don't know how many women he'd already tried that on. And there's a strong possibility he only did it to make me shut up, and that's just the kind of bizarre things people do at backstage gatherings, and I was way too smart to fall for any such lame come-on, and—oh . . . dang. It felt so good. I just stood there and giggled like a moron. I'd been on the road a long time, and something about this man's arms felt like home. I breathed in the scent of mountain snow and felt my blood oxygenating for the first time in possibly forever. It wasn't until he let go and stepped back that I recognized the brown-and-white wool worn by the man inside the snow globe.

He suggested we go for a walk.

"There's an occultation of Venus and Saturn tonight," he said. "If we walk out of town a little, it should be dark enough to see pretty well. It'll be cool. I'd really like to show you."

He seemed sincere. He also seemed very . . . *large.* (About six feet, four inches, I learned later, and almost 220 pounds.) But I had a can of Mace in my coat pocket, so I nodded, and we left the theater.

As we walked and talked about everything in the world, we discovered we had absolutely nothing whatsoever in common. He was ten years older than I—the difference between *Howdy Doody* and *Sesame Street.* When I talked about being close to my many brothers and sisters and my parents out West, he said he was raised out East and hadn't seen or spoken to his family in fifteen years. When I spoke about being into Stanislovsky, he informed me Method acting was "self-indulgent artsy horsecrap."

But he taught me the name of every constellation visible in the enormous night sky, and I taught him the words to a Leon Redbone song he liked. We covered world politics, vacant lots in the neighborhoods we grew up in and what you could do there in the summertime, what kinds of dogs we liked best, North Dakota jokes, Norwegian jokes, off-color jokes. We talked and laughed (he had a booming baritone laugh that was ticklish and rich and sweet as falling into a pile of hay) and walked and talked until four in the morning, then we walked for a while without saying anything, and then we stood still for a bit. And then we began searching desperately for anyplace warm enough to make love.

My idea was a hotel. Gary's idea was a snowbank.

The snowbank was closer.

"I don't know what I was thinking!" I lamented to Gwen the next day. "I'll probably never even see this person again."

That night, I was performing in a city two hundred miles away when I heard an unmistakably sweet baritone laughter from the dark audience.

"Say, um . . . you know that person you were never going to see again?" Gwen nudged me backstage. "He's here."

"*Oh, geez,*" I squeaked.

"Just relax," she warned in a whisper. "Don't get crazy."

"Too late."

Stepping back out onstage, I was newly nervous. I sang louder, tap-danced faster, and went for bigger laughs than I'd imagined I was capable of. When I came out of the dressing room after the final curtain, Gary was standing in the hallway with his hands in his pockets.

"Hey there," he said.

"Um . . . hey," was my witty and alluring response.

"So what are you doing after the show?" he asked.

"Oh, we—we've gotta go. We have to be in Jackson Hole by tomorrow."

"Ah. Well, I was thinking—if there's room on the bus . . . I mean, I could help load and strike the set or something . . . I've got a couple days off. . . ."

"Do you?"

"Oh, sure . . . yeah—well, no, actually. But I think I can arrange it."

"There's room," Gwen interjected helpfully.

Gary continued to follow me around the mountains as the tour went on through the winter and spring, meeting up with me here and there, making love to me in the seedy hotel rooms provided for the theater company. Whenever I had a few days off, I hitchhiked to Bozeman to be with him at his tiny cabin in Kelly Canyon. He bought a Scrabble game, and we sat for hours, playing out the wooden tiles near the woodstove.

Easter Sunday morning, we woke up to find snow piled so high the door couldn't be opened. It was one of the sweetest days of my life.

Now we were inside the snow globe together.

*T*here was a trout stream running by the back of the cabin, and Gary was standing there casting and reeling his line when I told him I was pregnant. I don't know what I expected him to say when I broke it to him by handing him a little rubber duck.

"But . . . you were on the pill," was what he did say.

"The doctor said it might have gotten messed up when I took antibiotics for that throat infection I had."

"Oh," he said, casting and reeling, casting and reeling.

We stood for a long time by the water. I twisted the front of my T-shirt in my hand.

"You said you loved me," I gently reminded him. "You keep saying you want us to spend our lives together . . . have children . . . be a family . . ."

"I did. I mean I *do*. But not *now*. Not like this. This isn't the right time or place for either one of us. I don't have the—the place . . . the money. You don't even have any insurance."

"Insurance?" I was incredulous. "You're talking to me about fucking *insurance?*"

"Fucking insurance," Gary huffed without humor. "There's a concept." He reeled the line in and puttered with the silver lure. "What about the show? If you don't stay with the tour, you won't be eligible for unemployment when the season ends."

"I don't know if I'll be able to finish the season. I was thinking I'd probably be hanging out here for a while. And then when—well, after the baby's born, I could get on at a radio station in Bozeman. I could do that."

"Yeah, you could, but what about—you talked about going back to school. We talked about traveling. What about all that?"

"We could still—"

"Oh, bullshit."

"We could!"

"And what if . . . physically—what if there's something wrong with it? You don't exactly live a healthy prenatal lifestyle. What did you tell the doctor about that?"

"I told her the truth. That I was drinking at first . . .

quite a bit and that . . . that I've been smoking some pot, but not that much, and that . . . that I've dropped acid a couple times."

He stared at me, surprised and hurt. Though he'd sown a bumper crop of wild barley hops himself when he was younger, Gary had settled into his thirties as dry as Carrie Nation. He liked to say he wanted to be "a clean machine." And so did I, but—well, what cleans better than alcohol?

"So much for my being a good influence on you," he said bitterly.

"You are, Gary, but I'm not here all the time, am I? I'm on the road, doing the show in a strange town with a bunch of people who expect me to be funny and sing loud and keep dancing—on stage and off."

"Fine, but did you have to have such a good time doing it?"

"Hey, I don't owe you any apologies. You weren't exactly sitting around playing Scrabble ten years ago when you were my age. You did your share of partying, too."

"Yes, I did! But I didn't bring a kid into the middle of it!"

"I don't want to bring a kid into the middle of it, either! That's not the lifestyle I want! I know that now. I want to stay here. With you. I want us to be . . . together. Just like you've been saying since the first day we met."

Gary tossed his lure back into the stream.

"So what did she say?" he asked.

"What?"

"The doctor. What did she say about all that?"

"They can't tell until later if it . . . if it had any effect."

He dropped the silver lure into his tackle box, picked up a green one, then gold. He weighed them in his hands, then put them away and closed the lid.

"Gary, I need you to do this with me. I'm certain I don't have what it takes to do this on my own."

"I don't want you to do it on your own, Joni. I want us to do it together. But *not now.*"

I couldn't tell if he was fighting tears or squinting against the flashing sunlight on the water. Suddenly, he clenched his fist against his forehead, then brought it down hard on the tackle box, denting the metal lid inward, and for the first time, I flinched away from him.

"I'm sorry," he choked. "I just can't do this right now."

I couldn't say anything. Couldn't swallow.

"I'm sorry," he repeated.

"So you keep saying."

I chucked the rubber ducky over his shoulder.

It splunked into the stream, bobbed, eddied, and drifted out of sight.

Several weeks later, we performed the last show of the tour at a resort in Ennis, but I had to be taken to the hospital after the second act. I never drank or smoked grass before a performance, but I was so hung over and dehydrated from the previous night that a slight case of the flu completely laid me out. After the abortion, I'd bled heavily, but because I couldn't bear to pass the protesters again, I never went back for the follow-up appointment where the doctor would have noticed I was becoming severely anemic. So, I lay on the emergency room gurney, watching the theater company bus drive down the road without me. I had no idea where I was going to go or how I was going to get there.

I awoke the next day to find Gary, sitting on the edge of a hospital-colored chair.

"Morning," he said, and when I didn't answer, he

moved the chair closer to the bed. "I ran into Gwen. She told me they left you here."

"Yeah. I guess they had places to go. People to see."

"So . . ."

"Right."

He walked over to the window and stood, looking out over the valley.

"How have you been?"

"How do you think?"

It was as green as it would get that year, but there was still snow on the mountains.

"What are you going to do now?" he asked.

"I'm not sure. Though of course, I am eligible for unemployment. *Huzzah.*"

If that hurt him at all, he didn't show it.

"Why don't you come and hang out at the cabin?" he asked after a bit.

"For how long?"

"Oh, I dunno," he grinned sheepishly. "Till death do us part?" When I didn't respond, he said, "Seriously, I think you should move over to Bozeman."

"What for?"

"So I can take care of you."

"Oh, that's nice," I laughed. "That's really big of you. But if there's one lesson I've learned here, it's that in sickness and health, for richer or poorer, I'm going to take care of myself from now on. It'll certainly be a cold day in hell before I ever depend on *you* for anything."

I saw his hands curl around the edge of the windowsill.

"I just want to know," he said evenly, "how long you're entitled to punish me for this."

"Oh, I dunno. Till death do us part?" But after a long

moment, I added, "It was my choice, anyway, not yours."

"It was the right thing to do," he said for the thousandth time. He'd said the same thing while it was being done. He'd held my hand while one nurse rummaged my wrist for a vein and the other lifted my legs into the stirrups. "It was the only thing that made any sense."

"Yes, I know, Gary. It's the first truly responsible decision I've made with my life. But somehow, knowing I made the right choice really doesn't make it any easier."

"No. It doesn't." He came back to the side of the bed and took my hand. "Look. Let me take you home and help you get your stuff, and then we'll see what happens. You know? You could just come for a couple weeks."

"Why should I?"

"Because I love you."

"Oh, yeah. Mm-hmm. I really believe that."

"Someday you will," he said. "I promise."

Gary returned the next day with a borrowed station wagon, and lacking any better suggestions, I agreed to go back to Bozeman with him and stay until Monday.

But just my dang luck. They had my favorite kind of soup at the Bacchus Pub on Tuesday. And Wednesday night, there was a concert in the park. Then Friday turned out to be perfect fishing weather, so I figured I might as well stay the weekend.

We were married the following September, among falling leaves and raised eyebrows, in a spur-of-the-moment, post-hippie, pseudo-Native American ceremony. Recognizing that one or both of us would back out if we were given too much time to think about it, we decided on a Thursday night to do the deed Saturday morning.

The only clergy we could clinch on such short notice was a tiny but dynamic woman who preached every Sunday morning from the roof of a local A&W Root Beer stand. She was scheduled to officiate at a wedding with a cowboy motif later that afternoon, so she was decked out in buckskin boots and a fringed leather jacket, topped off with a black Stetson hat that was bigger than our car.

We'd chosen the perfect setting, a babble-brooked clearing high in the Bridger Mountains, but we arrived—friends, dogs, and preacher in tow—to find our bucolic location already occupied by four yellow labs choke-chained to a silver Airstream trailer. Turns out it was the opening day of grouse season.

As we made our vows, shots rang out like Chinese fireworks.

Boom! BANG! Arf!

"... till death do us part."

A year later, we were living in the Midwest, working power-suit jobs and driving reliable cars. We had a house, a hibachi, and my parents' approval.

Never before or since have I been so unhappy.

Gary finally admitted he felt the same way. We'd left Montana so I could take a radio job, which paid me half again what Gary was making at his old job in Bozeman, and though he didn't consciously mean to punish me for that, he began to sink into himself. Conversation had become uncommon, sex sporadic at best. There wasn't a decent snowbank for miles.

Night after night, Gary sat there like a totem pole while I scrutinized and dissected every aspect of our relationship, finally coming to the conclusion it was pointless to pursue things any further. With no kids, and merely a moderately onerous amount of debt, it could have been mercifully quick for us to cut our losses.

My idea was a no-fault divorce. Gary's idea was to

answer a Peace Corps returnee newsletter advertisement seeking married couples and other two-person teams to staff lookout towers for the Forest Service.

"Well," I said, not taking him seriously, "after spending several months alone on top of a mountain, I guess any couple would either be happily married or happily divorced."

"No, seriously, we could do this," he insisted. "We could sell the cars and buy a truck—"

"Gary," I pointed out, "you're a chef and I'm a disc jockey. Neither one of us knows squat about the Forest Service."

"How hard can it be to distinguish between a tree that's on fire and a tree that's not on fire?" he countered.

"What about—what about our jobs—and this house—"

"Screw it! I'm not happy, you're not happy. Let's just say *screw* all of it and go."

This whole thing struck me as an uncanny reprise of that hotel versus snowbank issue. I'm still trying to figure out how he convinced me to do it. That and the snowbank. I am baffled still. But off we went, leaving our yuppie assets and ambitions behind us.

We were stationed on Weaver Bally, almost nine thousand feet up in the heart of Northern California's Shasta-Trinity Wilderness. The tower was another thirty feet high, a fourteen-by-fourteen wood-and-glass box with a steep staircase and narrow catwalk winding around the outside. Inside, there was a centered island for the maps and gauges, a little propane stove, and a wooden platform on which we spread our sleeping bags. Our only source of entertainment was a small boom box my father had given me. Our only communication with the outside world was a two-way radio with which we could call the Forest Service if we actually spotted a fire in what turned out to be the world's only nonflammable forest. We hauled a month's supplies up from town (the most useful of which turned out to be a cribbage board and cards), forgetting several important items (the most important of which turned out to be tampons) and allowing several others to be chewed up by deer while we were up in the tower, cleaning out the rats' nests.

The first day, a Forest Service truck lumbered up and filled a propane tank for the stove and lanterns, and a ranger named Chuck explained to us how to use the radio and spotting scopes. He indicated a spring located about three quarters of a mile down the road from which we would haul our water and pointed out his office, far away in the town below us, where we could come and pick up our mail if we were ambitious enough to trek down there once a month or so.

After he left, I set out to the spring with two five-gallon containers and an overabundance of self-confidence. On my way down the mountainside, I felt free and hopeful. Mount Shasta towered on the horizon, wild sage and green onions seasoned the breeze. I was Survival Woman: Fetcher of Water, Hydrator of All Good Things. At that moment, I truly believed that, through strength and determination, my man and I would carve a place for ourselves out of this wilderness, and emerge spiritually uplifted, our love revitalized, our marriage invincible. For the next seven months, we'd have nothing to do but boff our brains out.

Singing at the top of my lungs, I filled the containers and headed back to the tower. Fifty yards up the road, I paused and dumped a little water out of each container. Thirty yards farther, I dumped a little more . . . then a little more . . .

By the time I reached the foot of the fire tower, I had about three tablespoons of water left in each jug, my nose was gushing blood from the altitude, my arms were bitten bumpy by horseflies, and I wanted that divorce! Another good reason sprang to mind with every step I climbed to the catwalk.

Gary sat inside our house of glass, all unsuspecting, sighting and scoping out the territory with the Osborn Fire Finder.

"Hmm," he regarded my bedraggled form. "Didn't you get the water?"

"I really—really—h-hate you," I said between chest-wracking gasps of thin air. "You have ruined my life."

He wisely chose not to mention at that moment that, while I was gone, he'd blown up my boom box in an attempt to hot-wire it to a twelve-volt battery. In fact, he wisely chose not to say much of anything until late that night.

*H*ullo the house!" he called from a clearing at the base of the tower where he'd set up his telescope. I stepped out onto the catwalk, and he waved a flashlight. "Blow out the lamps and c'mon down."

Free of the streetlights and yard lamps of civilization, the darkness was a living thing; frightening at first, until Gary found my hand.

"The Orion nebula," he said, stepping away from the telescope and indicating the eyepiece.

"I don't see anything," I said, staring into it.

"You can't look directly at it. You can only see it with averted vision."

"How am I supposed to see something I'm not looking at?" I snapped.

"Just let your eyes drift and it'll happen."

I continued to squint and scrutinize for a while and finally gave up.

"I told you, I can't . . ." But the moment I started to turn away from the telescope, my eyes relaxed and the swirling blue nebula swam into sight, just as easy as falling in love.

Another cruel case of nature messing with my head.

When I originally agreed to make a life with this man, my sensibilities rushing and senses aflame, how was I to know staying in love was going to be so much work? With all that Bozeman snow in my eyes, it was tough to envision the trout streams and traffic jams to be waded through, the tax returns and dishes and dirty work to be done. We were so busy being in love, we'd completely forgotten to get to know each other.

I believe in love at first sight, but there are no shortcuts in marriage, no hacking into the Akashic record. Sooner or later, you have to do the work of building a relationship. Ours was a marriage made in heaven, but it took seven months in a box on a mountaintop for us to hammer out the logistics of living together on Earth. We came down at the end of the season, individually wiser and mutually more committed than when we went up. After a pre-agreed eight-week separation, we moved back to Montana together. I went back to the radio station and started teaching at Grandstreet. Gary went back to school to study aviation mechanics.

Over the years, the airline industry took us out East and then down South, but it also enabled us to travel west to Montana every summer. We had money, went broke, had fights, went for ice cream. We laughed, made love, had babies, and became a family.

*T*he day of my biopsy surgery, I slept until evening, then lay there eavesdropping while Gary put the kids to bed. I listened to him saying prayers with them, telling them I was fine, but they would have to be careful hugging me for a few days. After I heard him come out to the kitchen and put on a pot of coffee, I got up, groggy and hungover from outpatient anesthesia.

"Morning," I yawned.

"Hi."

He sat down in the wooden rocker and plugged PGA European Golf Tour into the Sega.

"You know," I teased, "the only thing more boring than playing golf is *pretending* to play golf. That takes the plaid pants mentality to a whole new level."

He grunted some monosyllabic response.

"So . . ." I said. "Guess we get the biopsy results at his office Friday, huh."

"Right."

"Well. That'll be a relief. To know. One way or the other."

"Yeah."

"And it could still turn out to be nothing, you know. It could turn out to be okay." When he didn't answer, I asked, "Did you eat supper?"

"Huh-uh."

"Do you want me to fix you something?"

"No thanks."

I meandered around the room, picking up small shoes and action figures, trying to start conversations about politics, the price of avocados, whatever. The Sega plinked and beeped softly. The program even had little golf course birdies twittering in the trees. Gary sat, staring at the virtual fairway, looking like a travel poster for Easter Island.

"What is *with* you?" I finally knelt down in front of him. "Talk to me."

In his face, there was a moment of struggle between his feelings and a need to be the Rock of Gibraltar. Then he crumpled forward, his head on my shoulder, his broad back heaving with sobs. He was holding me so hard I could barely breathe.

"What did they tell you?" I heard myself ask, but he couldn't answer and didn't have to.

We eventually lay down together later, but neither of us slept until dawn was already coming on. Beyond grieving for myself, I was heartsick and furious at the unspeakably cruel position the surgeon had put Gary in by telling him before he told me.

Toward morning, we dozed, and I dreamed I was on the fire tower, waking up to that dirigible's view of the Trinity Alps. The feeling of flying was so real, I was surprised and disappointed to open my eyes and discover the white walls of our apartment. I heard the sound of the shower shutting off, and Gary came out of the bathroom a moment later.

"Hi," he said.

"Morning."

"I'm sorry about . . . what happened last night."

"Gary, don't be. I want you to feel like you can be—"

"No. I want you to know that's not going to happen again. I want you to believe that I'm here and everything's cool and . . . that's not going to happen again. I'm going to make this be okay for you."

"Gary, you don't have to—"

He stepped back into the bathroom and closed the door.

We spent the next three days in the library and bookstore, and as I learned more about lymphoma, I realized that, had Gary not bulldozed through the managed-care maze on my behalf, my prognosis would have been extremely poor.

This type of cancer is "swift and virulent, fatal in six to twelve months," one source said. I was diagnosed four months after I first felt the lump, which had been growing quite some time before I felt it.

I had my first appointment with Dr. Ro right after Thanksgiving weekend and returned the next day for the longline installation, two bone-marrow aspirations, and my first blast of chemo.

It's the right thing to do, I told myself as a nurse prodded the back of my hand for a new vein from which to draw blood. *It's the only thing that makes any sense.* But I wondered if it was the ultimate act of faith or the ultimate lack thereof that led me to once again sacrifice a part of myself in order to preserve one narrow vision of the future. And I couldn't help noticing Gary was still holding my hand.

On a typical chemo day, he arrived home from work at 7:00 A.M., drove me to the clinic an hour from our home, picked up my prescriptions, and napped in a chair for a few hours while I got my blood work and received the treatment du jour. Then he drove me home, put me to bed, cleaned out whatever receptacle I'd used for vomit in the car, met the school bus, made dinner, fed the kids, put them to bed at eight, and left at eight-thirty to work all night again.

She's so brave, people said, as I stumbled through long months of chemotherapy. What a great attitude, what an inspiration. For the general public, I maintained a veneer of wisecracking good spirits. Only Gary had to deal with the deep chasm of panic and sorrow underneath. No one ever told him how brave he was, but he never wavered or complained. He just kept on bicycling through the blizzard.

The National Coalition for Cancer Survivorship has published a Patient's Bill of Rights, which states, among other things, that we are not obligated to act any more upbeat than we really feel. And I was so grateful, because really, that big yellow smiley face plastered to the front of my head got a little too heavy sometimes, and I had to sink into the mire. But I began to think there should be a Caregiver's Bill of Rights, too.

You have the right to remain silent, especially if every conversation is focused on cancer.

You have the right to serve pancakes for supper.

You have the right to not laugh at the cancer jokes.

*H*ey, Gary, why is chemotherapy like a vacuum cleaner? Because you plug it in and it sucks!"

Oddly, the people who laugh at the cancer jokes are generally people with cancer. (Maybe we're the ones who are least afraid of it.)

"Hey, Gary," I tried again, "why didn't the home health nurse cross the road? Because the chicken's HMO wouldn't approve it!"

I told that one to the home health nurse, and she didn't laugh, either. But Christine, the home health Nazi, didn't laugh at much of anything. Nurse von Helsing, as Gary affectionately referred to her, seemed to feel my cancer was some kind of personal affront to her. Like I'd gone and got myself all cancered up just to piss her off. She had a stern set of ideas on how I should be thinking, feeling, and forging ahead at any given moment, never mind that this was my body, my life, my cancer, and my right arm.

My right arm. My *right* arm. My right *arm*.

It was her opinion that I should have an extension on the longline that would enable me to shoot up my own heparin and saline at night.

"I'd rather not," I said. "It's so bulky, I can hardly play guitar or type as it is, and my husband always does the flush before he goes to work."

"And what are you going to do if he doesn't come home one morning?" she said, spreading out the sterile blue paper on the table under my arm.

"What?" I made a nervous little laugh.

She peeled the Primapore away from my cath port site and tore open the various supply packets so she wouldn't have to touch them after she snapped on her sterile latex gloves. Gauze pad, alcohol wipes, Betadine swabs, alcohol swabs, antibiotic salve, heparin and saline syringes, needles, surgical tape.

"I see a lot of women end up alone in this situation," she shrugged. "You need to be as independent as you can."

I glanced toward Jerusha, who'd come to the dining room to watch the gory procedure and was now hanging on every word.

"He'll be home," I said.

"You'd like to believe that," she smiled and swabbed my sutures with thick yellow Betadine, moving in a precise pattern outward from the site so as to maintain sterility. "But I'll bet I could name five women I see on a regular basis whose chemo is going to outlast their marriage. Unfortunately, the man usually leaves the kids and takes the health insurance with him."

"Well, that's not going to happen here."

"I see it all the time," she nodded at me knowingly. Conspiratorial.

I wanted to smack her. Partly because she was saying these things in front of my daughter. Partly because I could name five women I saw on a regular basis whose chemo had already outlasted their marriages.

"He didn't physically leave until I was in remission,"

one of them had told me. "But the day I was diagnosed, he started grieving, and by the time I got my first remission, he'd already let go."

"Cancer seems to put a magnifying glass on things," said another, "and a lot of relationships just don't stand up to that kind of scrutiny. I realized my life meant too much to me to settle for less than complete love."

"Men are shit," another uncharitably maintained. "I'm better off with the cancer."

"This was supposed to be my day off," Christine sighed, swabbing off the Betadine with alcohol wipes.

"Oh?" I didn't know what she wanted me to say.

"I was only supposed to be on call."

"Well . . . sorry. These sutures aren't healing because my white count is low. She said to get it changed every day until the infection—" I winced when the brusque motion of the alcohol wipe yanked painfully on the anchor plate sutured to my arm. She placed a gauze pad over the site where the tubing entered the vein and peeled open another Primapore, even though there were still yellow clouds of Betadine across my forearm. "Could you umm . . . see—the Betadine kind of irritates my skin so—if you could . . . you know . . . try to—to get it all . . . please?"

"I already have my gloves off," she rankled. "I can't go back to the sterile field unless I start all over again."

"Oh."

"It's just Betadine. It doesn't hurt anything."

"It's just—I'm sorry . . . I guess my skin is kind of sensitive. It really burns after a while. I need you to get it all."

"It doesn't hurt anything," she repeated, making no motion toward another pair of gloves. "And I really don't have time to start over. I'm taking my son to the movies at three. It's supposed to be my day off."

A Joni with more energy would have told her, *Screw your day off, honey. I've got freakin' CANCER, and I don't get a day off from that, do I?* But I just sat there, wondering which would be more draining, to squawk like a fishwife now or fume about it after she was gone.

"There." She made the decision for me by placing the Primapore and strapping a swatch of surgical tape across the whole shootin' match. "And here's the extension. See? It's not so bad."

"Take it off," I said.

She coiled the extra tubing and taped it to my wrist.

"Why don't we leave it until tomorrow and see how it feels?"

"Because we won't be back tomorrow," I told her with an equal dose of saccharine. "In fact, *we* won't be coming back at all. Because there's enough pain and aggravation in my life right now without *us* sitting here slopping Betadine all over and bitching about our bloody day off."

"Well," her eyes iced over, "it's fine with me if you want to drive all the way down to the clinic every day."

"I won't need to. The subcutaneous injections I can give myself, and Gary can do the rest."

"I'm sorry, we don't allow that."

"You don't *allow?* There seems to be some confusion about our relationship, Christine. I'm paying money for a service rendered. That makes me in charge of what's allowed and what's not."

"Joni, I know this is an emotional time," she patronized, "and I understand how you must feel—"

"I doubt it."

She started to answer, but I put my hand on hers.

"Look, Christine," I said softly enough to diffuse her sputtering, "I'm not mad. I'm not going to call the office looking for your head on a stick. But I don't want you to come back, because basically—I just don't like you. I don't like some of the things you say in front of my daughter, I don't like this extension, and I don't like the idea of spending what could be my last days on Earth hassling over it. So, please . . ." I stretched my arm out on the table. "Please take off the extension and clean up the Betadine so I don't have to call your boss and have her send someone else over here to do it. That would just be a drag for both of us."

When she'd finished, she gathered her stethoscope and blood pressure cuff, zipping her kit as tightly as her lips. As I showed her to the door, she suggested I get some counseling to deal with what was obviously deep-seated anger about my disease, and I thanked her for her concern.

Okay, I thought, *that felt like a reasonable compromise between fuming and fishwifery.*

Later, it occurred to me I probably should have asked Gary before I volunteered him for M*A*S*H duty. He paled a little at the suggestion, but went to the clinic the next morning for a training session. He learned how to clean the IV site and change the dressing, how to disconnect the Adriamycin pump, and how to inject me with white-count boosters. Donning a surgical mask and latex gloves that fit his wide hands like shades of the O.J. trial, he memorized the complex protocol like a chapter from the Bible and executed his tasks meticulously. He was gentle and thorough, starting all over again every time the sterile field was compromised by a sneeze or a cough or an accidental touch.

"Okay. This is going to hurt you more than it hurts me," he teased, drawing Neupogen from a small brown vial.

"Well, do I at least get a cookie or something when you're through?"

"Damn it, Jim, I'm a doctor, not a pastry chef!"

Gary held the syringe up to the light, expressing a few drops at a time until he had the precise dosage. I stuck out my arm, but he shook his head. I pointed hopefully to the front of my thigh, but he made a circling gesture with his finger.

"Large muscle injection, baby. Turn around and drop those drawers."

"You're not getting some kinky little pleasure out of jabbing me in the backside, are you?" I asked, lowering my britches.

"Are you kidding?" He snapped the side of the syringe to make sure there were no minute air bubbles. "I've been dreaming of this moment for years."

I've always been one of those people who keeps their cool during a crisis, then disintegrates immediately after. With the end of chemotherapy came an unexpected depression. I had the energy of a limp gnocchi, the charm of a toxic waste dump. I was still as bald as a baboon's backside, but not quite as attractive. My body was a Super Fund cleanup site, my theater career extinct, our children clingy and traumatized.

Our savings, such as it was, had been sucked down the drain in the first few months. We struggled for a while to keep our heads above water, but the steady barrage of "pay up or get out of the universe" notices were more than I could stand, under the circumstances. Finally accepting the inevitable, we declared bankruptcy, all our plans for the future vaporized by sobering statistics and overwhelming expenses.

As we stood before the judge, he asked us what our reasons were, and neither of us could put it into words.

"I have cancer," I finally stated the obvious. "I haven't

had any income for quite a while now . . . and I don't want my husband to be left with these debts when . . . if I—"

"We want to be able to start over," Gary interrupted. "When my wife gets well again."

But I didn't get well again. As the weeks and months dragged by, my fear and frustration combined with the late effects of chemo, including the onset of premature menopause, crystallizing to a deep, green anger, and I turned that anger on Gary. Moods swinging like a flying trapeze, I was alternately abusive and apologetic, accusing him of causing my cancer, then crediting him with my survival.

"I wouldn't blame you," I told him during one of the apologetic moments. "I would understand if you had to escape from all this."

He drew my face upward between his hands, never flinching when his fingers brushed the scar on my neck.

"Where would I escape to?" he asked. "You're my whole life."

I put my arms around him, instantly teary eyed.

"And like they say," he added, "life's a bitch."

Several months after my last blast of chemo, we went to Gary's company Christmas party. He was actually wearing a suit, and I had a close-cropped, but legitimate, hairdo. It was Christmas. The food was free. Good cause for celebrating.

We sat with Melodie King and her husband, Bill, and the conversation stayed surprisingly—but blessedly—off the topic of cancer, centering instead on fishing in Montana, the academic achievements of our children, and life in general.

"Cheese it," said Gary. "Here comes the pope."

The CEO of the airline had entered the banquet hall and

was passing among his serfs and vassals, clapping a shoulder here, clasping a hand there. As he approached our table, Gary stood up and thrust his hand forward.

"Hey, Gordon, how are you?"

After the CEO had moved on, Gary sat down beside me again, and grinned, "I just shook hands with one of the richest men walking the face of the planet."

"He should be honored," I said, and I meant it. In fact, I was tempted to bounce a cheese cube off the back of his billion-dollar noggin and tell him so. *Hey! Armani guy! You just shook hands with the best, bravest man walking the face of the planet.*

The band struck up a Clapton cover tune, and for the first time in fourteen years, my husband asked me to dance.

The lead singer closed his eyes, fancying himself *Unplugged.*

"Would you know my name . . . if I saw you in Heaven?"

We were awkward; Gary unaccustomed to the moves and I still trying to find my way back into my altered body, but we swayed together for something as sweet, if not quite as long, as a lifetime.

Remission from cancer is like a slow dance with a good man. There's a heightened awareness. Moments become clarified. Uncertainty is suspended. And because you don't know how long it will last, you allow yourself to imagine it will last forever.

"I love you," Gary whispered against my cheek.

And if I could have spoken, I would have said, "I believe you."

11

Totally Depressing Low-down Mind-Messing Reverse Peristalsis Blues

> If I had use of my body, I would
> throw it out of the window.
>
> —SAMUEL BECKETT

*C*hemotherapy," my friend Sally shook her head sympathetically when I was first diagnosed. But then her face brightened. "You're gonna get so *skinny!*"

I won't lie. The thought had already crossed my mind. But to hear her say it out loud brought the true perversity of it to the conscious portion of my shiny little head. The idea that having cancer is preferable to being fat is obscene, but c'mon—everybody knows it's true. Just ask any of those women who refuse to quit smoking for fear of gaining weight. So emaciation is no longer a side effect. Thanks to Calvin Klein, it's now a perk. At some point in our cultural memory, the Rubinesque bounty of the Dutch masters went out and the fraline, suck-cheeked skeleton look came in. So after a lifetime of struggling to keep my weight within optimum range (give or take thirty pounds) I was thrilled to have a bright-eyed optimist like Sally point out to me that chemo toxins were just Jenny Craig with a very bad attitude.

Sadly, her sunny presage was not to be. Instead of getting fashionably ribby, I blimped out like a blowfish, because the first thing Dr. Ro did was pump me full of more steroids than the Estonian women's swim team.

They should print right on the bottle: PULL TO INFLATE.

I combined the Prednazone puffiness and chemically enhanced appetite with my own finely honed powers of rationalization, telling myself that, on the days I could eat, I deserved as much comfort food as a person could put away. I began to look like Shelly Winters in *The Poseidon Adventure*.

After I lost my hair, I figured I deserved as much comfort food as *three* people could put away. I began to look like Ernest Borgnine in *The Poseidon Adventure*.

In the first three months, I packed on more than forty pounds. And it's not that I didn't throw up. I threw up plenty. By my fourth cycle of chemo—well, I won't go into the indelicate details, but I am no longer welcome at Pancho's Mexican Buffet.

It amazes and amuses me that, in the American dialect, there are almost as many idioms pertaining to reverse peristalsis as there are pertaining to sex. We have, for some reason, developed about a thousand chow-blowing, lunch-losing, supperspewing ways to express this biological function we wouldn't be talking about in the first place, if we had any sense of decorum whatsoever. Perhaps it's our tendency to flirt with disaster; that roller-coaster reaction that makes us laugh at something that makes us feel kinda queasy at the same time.

What frat function does not resound with heroic epics of the guy who barfed on his girlfriend as they frolicked in flagrante delicto. You'd like to think women would have more class than that, but I remember a great deal of hilarity in the dorm when a stomach-churning splatter was discovered on the bathroom floor, and the drunken culprit was betrayed by the recognizable evidence of Chips Ahoy! cookies therein. Who hasn't laughed at apocryphal tales of the carsick child with the Little Mermaid backpack or the airsick passenger ("I told you—we're out of the chicken!") on the 747 or the time Petey Bukowski dropped his doughnuts in the middle of *Nightmare on Elm Street IX: Terror of the Mediocre Production Values.* Only one thing has the power to turn the IBM executives' charter fishing boat excursion into Beavis and Butt-Head's party adventure. It made Linda Blair famous while permanently lowering pea soup futures, and it rides shotgun to baldness as we cruise down the back alleys just off Chemo Boulevard.

Gary had a hard time seeing the humor in all this.

We were always prepared with a lidded container, damp cloth, and paper towels, but one fateful day, Captain Readiness placed these items in the trunk (possibly because his obdurate sidekick, Bravado Girl, left the clinic after a Bleo booster saying, "I feel fine, I tell you! Stop fussing over me!").

Gary hadn't eaten since the night before, and the proud claim of six billion served beckoned him off the highway and lured him to the crackly siren song of the McDrive-thru. He rolled down his window and called for a dead animal *avec fromage* and an extra large order of greasy McSpuds.

"Are you sure you don't want anything?" he asked, peeling back the wrap from his cadaver sandwich.

I shook my head. He pulled out into the rush-hour traffic, and maneuvering his way across the jamming lanes, bit into the grilled remains.

This may well be the moment I truly became a vegetarian. I later drew on the unforgettable impression to describe "the fetor of plastic orange cheese congealing with stage-blood ketchup and squirt yellow mustard over the greasy brown stench of fly-buzzing slaughterhouse cow carcass" in a book I was writing.

I seized the sorely inadequate paper bag and ralphed all over his crispy golden fries. This made me think for a fleeting moment about the Rialto in downtown Helena, where they used to serve fries with some kind of artery-choking gravy, and that made me hurl all over my raincoat.

Make that six billion minus one.

This incident in itself might not have provided as much amusement as it does now if not for the fact that later that same day, Gary offered to take the kids out for supper to spare me the smell of food in the house. Since our neighbor Vida had watched Jerusha after school, I suggested he might also take her little boy, Arturo. He was supposed to take them someplace reasonably non-junk oriented, but this brave man relented to their pleas of Jack-in-the-Box and fed them all cheeseburgers and fries.

"Oh dear," Vida said as Gary handed her Arturo's shirt with a pair of barbecue tongs. "You know, he told me his tummy hurt earlier. He must be coming down with something, poor baby."

$\mathcal{L}$ittle by little, the days I couldn't eat began to outnumber the days I could. Once I'd thrown up after eating something, I could no longer eat anything that smelled or looked like it. Unfortunately, the foods I was most likely to retain were sugar and empty calories—animal crackers, white bread, and applesauce—instead of vegetables, meat, or dairy products. I finally got to a point where virtually every victual known to the Food Channel had some awful regurgitative memory associated with it. Every aroma, every commercial, every aisle of the grocery store set my stomach rocking like a rowboat. I couldn't drive past a Shoney's billboard without feeling seasick. Eventually, the most I could manage was an occasional dry flour tortilla or half slice of bread.

The artificial feeling of being constantly and ravenously hungry faded into a more immediate ambience of light-headed nausea, and that became the state with which I was familiar, if not completely comfortable. I imagined myself fasting for spiritual nourishment, tried to pretend the cancer was giving me something instead of taking something away.

"How did you do this for three years," I asked one of my chemo buddies.

"Doobie, dear," she answered unequivocally. "Grass. Weed. Pot. I toked the Almighty Bong." (There's another one of those multiple idiom concepts.)

"Where did you get it?"

"Oh, I grew my own," she said. "You can't trust something you'd buy on the street. There might be something weird in it."

I was still contemplating the irony of that statement when she offered to send me some, but visions of Sniffy the Canine Cop barked in my brain, telling me that would be a foolish thing to attempt, especially with my name and address on the front of the package. When things got intensely bad, when I could no longer keep the Lorazipam down and the suppositories had only a mild, dulling effect on the dry heaves, Gary was determined to go out and find some reasonably safe marijuana for me to smoke, but I couldn't allow him to risk his freedom or his career. Drug tests were routinely performed at the hangar, and even secondhand smoke might have shown up in his urine.

"Yup," my chemo buddy commented dryly, "thank God we have the United States government looking out for our health. Can't have a bunch of potheads getting in the way of the industrial polluters who gave us cancer in the first place."

Ultimately, my only relief came from meditation. I discovered that, as with pain, fighting the nausea increased it. Instead, I learned to float on it, to give myself over to the feeling and accept it as part of the cauterizing process of chemotherapy. I still wasn't able to keep food in my stomach, but after a time, I was able to control the dry heaves. (In fact, I became so good at this method of deep relaxation, I can now cure myself of the hiccups in about fifteen seconds.)

From my fifth cycle of chemo until months after my final dose, I was able to eat virtually nothing. My weight dropped back somewhat, but my metabolism was pretty well in Park by that time. I still weighed a hefty 210 when my chemo was completed and my remission confirmed. With a statuesque six feet of height underneath me, I can carry a little extra weight, but a girl would have to be Hakeem Olajuwan to pull that off.

*M*y life became a quest for protein. Dr. Ro encouraged me to drink Ensure and, when I still wasn't able to eat after two or three months, sent me to a nutritionist. The nutritionist had wonderful advice for a well-balanced diet, of course, but didn't seem to recognize that it all hinged on one's ability to consume said diet without immediately tossing one's well-balanced cookies.

"The chemo shouldn't be affecting you anymore," she said. "There's probably some damage to the stomach lining, but other than that, no physical reason you can't eat."

I couldn't explain to her that some part of me—not my mind—didn't want to eat, didn't want to feed this enormous body, didn't want this enormous body to live. This body had betrayed me. Everywhere I looked, the people I loved were in pain, and this hulking androgenous barn I lived in was the cause. The last thing it deserved was a cappelletti fritter.

Janis introduced me to the Power Bar, and that helped. It was something I'd never eaten before, and so had never vomited. And it was ten grams of protein packed into one innocuous little plank.

That summer, I sat on the steps with a neighbor girl who was struggling with anorexia nervosa. As we talked, it started seeming terribly ironic that the two of us, me with my blowfish physique and Samantha with her skeletal one, had something very basic in common.

"Believe it or not," I told her, "I have a pretty good idea how you feel. Everybody around me is watching me, telling me to eat—"

"And getting mad at you when you don't," she nodded with tears in her eyes.

"They don't understand—I can't. They don't understand why, and they don't know how to help me—except to shove more food in my face."

"I wish I could explain all the elements that went into making me be this way." She shook her head, "But I don't understand it myself."

"Me neither," I told her. "But we will. Sooner or later." I took her delicate hand in mine. "Meanwhile, you and I, Samantha—we should make a pact. To live. Let's just agree to survive until all this crap has a chance to work itself out."

*M*y weight ebbed back a little further, then lumbered up to 220 as I discovered I could eat bread and pasta again. Every time I looked in the mirror, I felt more discouraged. I was heavier than I'd ever been in my life, and even as the rational part of my brain told me to rejoice in the fact that I was alive, my aching knees and back conspired with the general flabby malaise and post-cancer fatigue to make me almost wish I wasn't. With my remission came a profound depression. I had the unexpected sense of being abandoned by the cancer. It had brought me to this state and then left me, taking all my good excuses with it.

"I put on a lot of weight while I was in chemo," I'd mumble.

"Don't most people lose weight when they're in chemo?" was the skeptical response.

"Well, yeah, but I also just had a baby . . . six years ago."

Ultimately, of course, there is no excuse for being fat in this culture. It's the one last prejudice we allow ourselves, the final frontier of acceptable segregation. Our political correctness is positively Californian when it comes to race, creed, origin, and orientation. But we still condemn ourselves and others for this last intolerable offense in an annoyingly tolerant society. At least cancer had a certain melodrama about it. Obesity just takes up space.

My isolation, my humiliation, my self-destruction were complete. I was bald, I was barfing, I was yak-ass ugly, and I was *huge*. Godzilla in size 22 jeans. Every thundering step I took sent hoards of tiny little Japanese people scurrying. "I don't know what it is, but it's headed for the buffet! *Aaaaaaaaaaaaaaaaaaghh!*"

There could be only one source of salvation for me then. One wellspring of hope, one foundation upon which to resurrect my being, one fountain from which to draw my strength. The Omnipresent One who cries a woman's tears and feels a woman's thighs.

Richard Simmons.

*S*weatin' *to the Oldies* reminds me of that old joke about hitting yourself in the head with a hammer. (It feels so good when you stop.)

"C'mon and pony with us!" my videotaped tormentor chirps.

The pulsing cannibal drums of "Wipe Out" drive the obese of America onward. *Nyar-nyar-nyar neenur neenur neenur*, the electric guitars surf in, and he pumps his left knee up to his right elbow. My left knee and right elbow, having been lying on the couch, fat and fallow for several months, resist this procedure, but the flaming, frizzy-haired, little bastard doesn't seem to care.

"Other side!" he cries, left elbow to right knee now.

I do a few, then jog in place until he gets to a part I can keep up with. I remember a time before I was diagnosed when I commented to my friend Carole (who actually got a phone call from Richard Simmons one time) that *Sweatin' to the Oldies* was getting too easy for me. Now, by the time we get to "Great Balls o' Fire," I'm already burned-out.

But does the falsetto fascist take pity? No. He doesn't recognize what a good excuse cancer is. He doesn't appreciate how my limbs feel like lead, how the easy chair draws me like an electromagnet. He doesn't see why I should be allowed to quit, doesn't seem to understand that I am worthless, telling me instead that I am beautiful, if slightly imperfect, but would, of course, be even better if I were healthier. Stronger. If I thought more highly of myself.

I've never met Richard Simmons. Never talked to him on the phone. Wrote him a couple letters, but felt too silly to mail them. He doesn't know anything about me or this manic love-hate relationship I have with him, and this is why I trust him so implicitly. He and Dr. Ro were the only ones who expected me to pick up the pieces and get on with the business of being alive. Everyone else seemed to have gotten used to the idea of me being dead. And in the blue-black funk of depression I sank into, my VCR was the only one with the stamina to spend any time with me. People who knew me figured I had an excuse to look like hell, so why fight it? People who loved me felt so sorry for all my poor body had been through, they didn't have the heart to harangue, "C'mon! Eight more!"

But to Richard Simmons, I was just another fat chick. He's the only one who treats me now the same way he treated me BC, and he serves an important dual role in my life; exercise guru and whipping boy.

Excreting toxic sweat from every pore, I castigate and cuss him for all the sins of this inequitable world, venting on him all the frustration I feel toward society in general and my own body in particular. Unexpectedly, the venting feels as cathartic as the sweat, as curative as the chemo. As I unload all my fat and my frustration upon him, I discover I have reversed an old dilemma; I used to be addicted to food and hated exercise—now, I hate food and I'm a workout junkie.

"Take it easy," I try to tell him. "I've been sick."

"Once more!" he cries. Grimacing grins in place, his dimpled video disciples comply.

"Oh, please," I pant. "Not again. . . ."

"And again!"

". . . no more . . ."

"Four more!"

"I can't do it."

"You can do it!"

Casting aside all Hamlet's advice, the sadistic little tart flings, bounds, saws the air, prancing a sideways grapevine, dragging me and my fifty extra pounds along with him.

"C'mon! We're gonna pony again!"

"Die, Pony Boy, die!"

"Bongo arms!"

"Up yours, you beady-eyed hairball from hell!"

But I bongo.

12

Being a Phoenix

Barn's burnt down—
Now, I can see the moon.

—MASAHIDE

*T*ake a deep breath and hold it."

Red light. *Whrrrrrrrrr.*

"You may breathe."

Green light.

"Take a deep breath and hold it."

The CAT scan ritual is a curious combination of heavy machinery, Velcro restraints, radioactive dye, and garments that open down the back. Not the most fun a person could have while tied to a table. It could almost be a kinky holdover from the days of the Spanish Inquisition if not for the piped-in BeeGees music and tutti-fruity taste of barium.

Prior to the procedure, there's a long list of questions to be answered. I'm not sure why they can't consult previous copies of the same questionnaire I've already responded to each of the twenty or so times I've undergone this procedure.

Probably a union thing. One of the more oddball inquiries is "Do you routinely eat shellfish?" They actually ask this because the iodine in the contrast injection can cause anaphylactic shock in people who are allergic to shellfish, but it still makes me feel like I'm being interviewed for one of those computer-dating services. I suggested once that perhaps they should ask if I routinely listen to BeeGees music, which I'm certain could also cause anaphylactic shock, but the technician just looked at me for a moment and then asked, "Are you or have you ever been claustrophobic?"

I always say no. I don't want to sound like a big wimp. And the truth is I never have been, but the first few times they fed me into the narrow white corridor, I lay for the next forty-five minutes with my heart in my throat. Perhaps that's why they continue the hypnotic drone of breathing instructions rather than simply say, "Green light means breathe, red light means hold it" right at the get go. It bothered me less after I had a MUGA scan, an Edgar Allan Poe experience that involved being sandwiched between two metal plates and lying motionless for an hour and a half after drinking about eight gallons of radioactive contrast agent. From that day on, the CAT scan felt roomy as the Ritz.

"Take a deep breath and hold it."

Red light. *Whrrrrrrrrr.*

"You may breathe."

Green light.

"Take a deep breath and hold it."

Lagenia told me once that it took three years of remission before she could bring herself to buy a winter coat. She just wasn't quite convinced she'd still be around when the season changed. When I finished my chemo, I experienced that same *what now?* feeling.

Sitting in Dr. Ro's office on day one of my last chemo

cycle, I felt like a puppy about to be tossed out of the litter. Dr. Ro was pleased with the results of recent scans and was ready to move on.

"All righty then!" Gary was ready to move on, too. "Now, the radiation—"

"No," I said. "No radiation. According to the reading I've done, the possible benefits aren't worth the risk of destroying my voice."

"What? What about the risk of destroying your *life?*" Gary argued. "I know the idea of the radiation is scary, but—"

"Gary, I was scared of the chemo, too. But I took it because I could see that it was my best hope. Radiation on my neck could permanently—"

"I don't care! The statistics say you've got a better chance of long-term survival with chemo *and* radiation."

"I'm going to make up for it by doing what I should have been doing all along—taking care of myself. Spiritually and physically. I'm going to stop eating red meat, cut way back on sugar. I'll keep meditating and exercising . . ."

We both looked to Dr. Ro, and I was amazed and grateful when she came out on my side.

"The radiation," she said carefully, "would be a prophylactic measure. The chemo itself appears to have been as effective as we could have hoped for. And if there should be a reoccurrence, there are many rescue measures still available to us."

"Okay," I said. "Good. Then . . . I'm done? That's it?"

"That's it," she smiled. "I'll see you in one month for bloodwork, examination, and CAT scans. Then we'll wait two months, then I'll see you every three months for a year, then we'll make it every six months for five years and once a year for five years after that."

"And then . . . I'm cured."

"We say 'cured' after ten years," she nodded, "because the likelihood of reoccurrence after that time is very small. For now, we call it 'remission.'"

Hearing her say these things, I wanted to feel joy, but I didn't. From the beginning, I'd had one objective: remission. Somehow, in my mind, "remission" meant "okay." I'd thought I would be celebrating, dancing around the room singing a la *Fiddler on the Roof*, "Re-mi-shaaaaaahn—RE-MI-SHUN!" It hadn't occurred to me I'd be doing *Cabaret* instead; "Good-bye to you, mine hair!" It hadn't occurred to me that I would be bald, bloated, and miserable, that my energy would equal that of a sea slug, and I would not be, in any sense of the term, *Okay*.

It hadn't occurred to me that the return journey from Planet Cancer would be almost as turbulent and twice as lonely as the first leg of the trek.

When Dr. Ro turned to leave the room, I wanted to throw my arms around her and cry, "Don't go!" like Jerusha used to do when I tried to abandon her to the uncharted menaces of her preschool classroom.

"Take a deep breath and hold it."

Red light. *Whrrrrrrrrr.*

"You may breathe."

Green light.

"Take a deep breath and hold it."

The hot flashes hit me while I was visiting my sister Janis in San Jose for the weekend. Janis's house is usually very therapeutic for me, but I couldn't get comfortable. I gravitated between the cool of the arbored patio and the warmth of the fireplace and changed my clothes five times a day. Dr. Ro had explained early on that premature menopause is a common aftereffect of chemo. She hadn't mentioned it was going to feel like spontaneous human combustion.

"Take a deep breath and hold it."

Red light. *Whrrrrrrrrr.*

I dreamed I had a beautiful snake in a large aquarium. My sisters were coming to my house, but just before they arrived, I was horrified to discover the living room floor was crawling with rats and roaches. I released the snake who rapidly ate them all, striking so quickly, it was almost invisible, just a blur at the corner of my eye as I opened the door, invited them in, carried on the pleasant conversation. My sisters never noticed. When they went into the kitchen, I tried to put the snake back in the aquarium, but when I tried to catch it, it bit me on the arm. I seized its head and pulled it away from the wound, but it was very powerful, much larger than I thought it was. I looked at my arm and saw two distinct holes where it had sunk its fangs in just above my wrist. As I watched, my skin began to take on the colors and texture of the snake. Instead of being afraid, I was thrilled at how beautiful my arm was now; red and black and gold and incredibly supple and strong. But then the arm began to feel paralyzed, as dream limbs do, and the hand in which I held the snake began to feel weaker and weaker. I could hear my sisters coming, laughing and talking, but I hid, not wanting them to know what I was becoming. The snake strained and flexed in my hand, stretching its open mouth toward my face. It was almost level with my eye.

"You may breathe."

Green light.

"Take a deep breath and hold it."

Red light. *Whrrrrrrrrr.*

"You may breathe."

Green light.

"Take a deep breath and hold it."

One day, I had harsh words with the assistant principal

of the elementary school. Malachi was involved in a typical third grade behavior incident, and the assistant principal told me an example needed to be made demonstrating their zero-tolerance policy toward fighting. This meant that Malachi would be sent to in-school suspension for five days, right along with the little boy who clobbered him.

Now, I'm not generally a confrontational person. I can go with the flow, I can move with the groove. I can be diplomatic when I choose to be, but when it comes to my children, I tend to come out à la barracuda. Buoyed by a snootful of steroids, I verbally ground her to Spam, and Malachi was back in class the next day. (Important safety tip for public education administrators: artificial hormones and petty bureaucratic bullshit don't mix.)

The next day, as I lay strapped inside the CAT scan machine, I came to the sickening realization that I was happy to be there instead of facing the fallout of real life. Returning to the metal womb, I knew exactly what was expected of me. And it wasn't much.

"Take a deep breath and hold it."

Red light. *Whrrrrrrrrr.*

"You may breathe."

Green light.

"Take a deep breath and hold it."

Cancer treatment insulated me with solid walls of special circumstance. For months, I'd been hiding inside that fortress where caregivers hovered, detractors deferred. Extenuated from all the rules that govern the daily grind, I had my mother to take care of me, and when I didn't have her, I had the mother of all excuses. But now the drawbridge had dropped, and all my old problems were waiting patiently on the farside of the moat, armed with the added battering ram of post-cancer fatigue. Nonetheless, everyone was looking at me, saying, "So come on, already. Bounce back! Get over it! You're in *remission!*"

Gary wanted a house. He was never really cut out for apartment community living. ("I'm not one of those people meant to be stacked up like cord wood!") But more than that, he wanted to feel something solid under his feet after the firm foundation he'd thought he was living on turned out to be more like a Jell-O mold. Texas is extremely forgiving when it comes to matters financial, so despite our bankruptcy, we knew we'd be able to qualify for a standard mortgage in eighteen months or less. Gary was determined to find a lease-purchase deal on his American dream, and though I was as eager to leave the apartment complex as he was, I still felt pretty much like a renter in the housing project of life. Lagenia's old winter coat thing, I guess. I couldn't see anything as permanent as home owner-ship applying to me. Some days, I couldn't see anything as permanent as Scotch tape applying to me.

"This isn't the right time," I tried to tell him as he dragged me on yet another expedition through the shady streets of yet another subdivision. "I'm lying in the middle of the road, watching this bus that just hit me disappear around the bend. I need some time to—"

"We need to get everything back to normal," he insisted. "Nothing's changed."

"Everything's changed, Gary! *I've* changed! And since when was anything ever 'normal'? There's no such thing as normal."

"Hmmm." He slowed to crawl past a fake Tudor with a yard ornament that looked like a little old lady's backside sticking up. "Add a couple pink flamingos, and that could be it."

*F*our months after my last Bleo booster, in a genuine attempt to get things back to that ever elusive "normal," I made my annual pilgrimage to Montana. In the high, clean air, my hot flashes seemed to abate somewhat. I rejoiced in seeing the mountains I'd been so afraid I'd never see again, and my father rejoiced in seeing me for the same reason.

Driving down Last Chance Gulch toward the No Sweat Café my second morning in town, I saw Jon walking out of Rock's Western Bar, and I honked and waved.

"Jon!"

"Well, hey!" he called and started to cross the street toward me, but the light turned green and the car behind me revved impatiently.

"Get in," I called, pushing the passenger-side door open. He dove in, and I hastily hugged him before continuing up the Gulch.

"Well . . . hey," he said again.

"Do you have time for coffee?" I asked.

"Oh . . . no. I should probably . . ."

He was looking at me oddly, and I was conscious of my hat and scarf in the backseat of the rental car. I wasn't exactly bald anymore, but I still looked like a Pro-Cuts poster child.

"My classes don't start till next week, but I thought I'd run up to the theater and say hello to everybody," I said. "I was just going to stop by the No Sweat on my way if you have time for—"

He took in a deep breath. "Joni."

"Yeah." There was an awkward silence. "Do you always go hopping right into the cars of women you don't recognize?"

"Only the ones who ask me."

We laughed, and that helped a little.

"Well." I parked the rental car in front of the café. "So . . ."

"It's good to see you," we both said at the same time, and then both nodded uncomfortably.

"Listen, I'm sorry I haven't called," he started. "You know how time just—"

"It's all right," I shrugged. "Truth be told, a lot of my friends have been conspicuous by their absence in the last year. I understand, though. It's okay."

"So . . . how are you," he asked. "Are you . . . I mean—you look . . . you look really . . ."

"I look like it beat up on me pretty good," I said, wanting to help him out. "But everything's going to be all right."

That was my tenth summer at Grandstreet. Dr. Ro had tried to tell me it might be overambitious, planning to go ahead and teach the first- and second-grade beans, but all year I'd been reassuring Marianne, the theater school director, that I might not look too great, but I would absolutely, positively, most definitely be there. The commitment had provided one of my most powerful chemo chair visualizations—the image of myself, strong and healthy, playing Quacknoodles with the little beans and leading them up Last Chance Gulch in the children's parade. After all, I was in remission. Remission equals okay, right?

Just to prove it, I showed up at orientation wearing an enormous strawberry blond bouffant wig and a fantabulous pair of red cat's-eye sunglasses.

Thank God, Linda's fifteen-year-old daughter, Lorna, a longtime Grandstreet kid and blossoming theater maven, was selected to be my assistant for the two-week session. She and Nancy, the kindergarten-group teacher, took the two classes of about twenty children each through the children's parade route without me. Linda stayed at the theater until 2:00 A.M., gluing construction-paper crabs, clown fish, and sea anemones onto a backdrop while I lay on the floor nearby. Mom took care of Malachi and Jerusha and helped with costumes for my grand musical adaptation of the Beatles' *Yellow Submarine*, a titanic production that was supposed to demonstrate to everyone I was back with flying colors.

After Sgt. Pepper's Lonely Hearts Club Band rallied the people of Pepperland and vanquished the Blue Meanies, Apple Bonkers and all, the children sang out the final number with great gusto.

There's nothing you can sing that can't be sung . . .

I realized my class was now populated with the children born to me and my friends during one of those little baby booms a community of friends will sometimes experience. Jerusha played His Blueness, the Grand High Meanie. Nancy's daughter, Emily, was Admiral Fred. Marianne's baby Josie (wasn't she a baby just five minutes ago?) played the Dreadful Flying Glove.

Nothing you can do but you can learn how to be you in time . . .

In the audience sat a ladder of little beans I'd taught over the years. Some were in middle school now, some were about to graduate high school, and they all joined in on the chorus.

All you need is love. . .

It felt like a circle. But as the circle closed, I felt myself standing outside of it.

At the end of the day, I told Marianne I wouldn't be back.

Sid was in remission, too. When we saw each other in Helena, she was getting her wild mane of curly hair back, and she seemed to be the same wonderful Sid she'd been before.

"So what have you done with your book lately?" she asked me.

"I did a lot of rewriting while I was in chemo," I said. "And I've cultivated a fabulous collection of rejection letters."

"How many?"

"About twenty-five." It was actually more like fifty. "Some say it's too long. Some don't like the lesbians, some don't want to get into the political issues, it's too literary to be called a romance, too commercial to be called literary fiction, too much Montana, not enough Montana. Everybody thinks it's too long. Mostly they send the 'does not meet our needs at this time' letter. But I haven't sent anything out for about six months."

"Well, get off your ass, girl! It's an incredible book, better than the vast majority of what's out there." This meant something to me, coming from a librarian. "So you can sit there with your twenty-five rejections and a box of paper, or you can go for fifty rejections and a published manuscript."

"Part of the problem is—well, Gary's not too keen on the idea of spending more money on querying. He wants me to get a normal job. A secretary job or something where I'll get a regular paycheck and—and we can all . . . we can all be happy."

"Can you be happy?"

"I don't think so."

"Then don't do it. Haven't you figured it out, girl? This was your wake-up call. Life is precious. Life is short. And all those other clichés. You can't afford to spend any more time doing what other people want you to do."

"I know, but . . . I'm not sure I have the stomach for any more rejection right now," I confessed. "I'm feeling kind of fragile."

"You got those other rejections because it wasn't the

right time. Not the right time, not the right place. No great loss. The book is good. Somebody's going to recognize that."

You see why I continue to invest my long-distance dollars in this woman?

I furtively organized another round of queries, including the usual cover letter and bio propaganda along with the first three chapters. I'd started writing a second novel while I was still in chemo, and ideas for scenes and dialogue continued to crowd the back of my head, so I created a computer file with the large heading FAMILY BUDGET at the top and a macro that allowed me to hit shift F3 and instantly switch to the dummy spread sheet if Gary came into the room while I was working on it.

"Whatcha doin', babe?"

"Oh . . . just . . . you know." I'd indicate the fake screen.

"I wish you wouldn't worry so much about that," he'd say, rubbing my shoulders and heaping hot coals of guilt on my head. "It'll work itself out."

I felt like pond scum, both for doggedly pursuing something so futile and for being dishonest with him. There was no court proceeding I knew of that could begin to discharge the enormous debt I owed this man, but a new, disjointed dynamic had evolved in our relationship. Slowly but surely, I'd given over to Gary all the responsibilities and privileges I simply didn't have the energy to carry. Now, I found myself feeling I was no longer entitled to voice an opinion, and I had a sad suspicion Gary had grown to like it this way. He had to do more of the work, but he held all the power. There were no more pleasantly heated arguments, no zinging comebacks. I was easy.

Several times, I tried to stop working on my books, packed them in boxes and buried them in the bottom of the coat closet. But they weren't about to go gently, either.

This would be the last round of queries, I resolved, putting together six packages, each addressed to a small-to mid-size publisher whose books I'd seen and liked. I kissed each envelope, pressed it to my forehead with a silent prayer and handed it to the postal worker. She looked at me doubtfully (though you'd think a postal worker would be the last one to cast aspersions on someone else's mental stability), and it occurred to me that after a total of five dozen rejections, I might do well to reevaluate this good-luck ritual.

Over the next few months, all six publishers responded with requests for the full manuscript, but by this time, the book had swollen to the size of Mama Cass, and I could only afford to print two copies. After a little more homework, I selected the two most likely candidates and shipped off the tomes in cookie boxes. The silence was deafening. I might as well have air-dropped them into the Bermuda Triangle.

*H*ey," Gary pointed to an item in the Sunday paper. "Did you see this call for auditions for Christmas Revels? That's just like that production you did in Pennsylvania. You should call."

I had seen it and had already worked up a fresh excuse for not going. It had been well over a year since I'd auditioned for anything, and I found the very idea of dragging myself to some cattle call so I could be compared to a bunch of younger, thinner, healthier women was about as appealing as a time-share in a Turkish prison. It didn't seem possible at first—that the desire to do theater was no longer part of my biology, but I was seriously overweight, and my once-powerhouse voice had been weakened by the damage Bleomycin did to my lungs.

Gary began to gently but persistently press me to audition for commercials or apply for temp work. Money was painfully tight, and after four or five months, he started asking, "Um—no pressure, of course—but, well . . . how long is it going to be like this?"

I had no answers for him. I didn't know where I was headed, but I was certain I couldn't go back to where I was before.

I stopped working on the second novel. There didn't seem to be much point with the first one still sitting somewhere in a box. I was invited to substitute teach for the school district, but couldn't bring myself to go in for the TB test. When school started, I put Malachi and Jerusha on the bus each morning and went back to bed. Gary tried to interest me in poking through antique stores or going out to lunch, but most days, I just felt like napping.

"So . . ." I said grimly to Dr. Ro as she renewed my lease on life for another sixty days. "I guess I lived."

"Why do you sound sad when you say that?" she asked.

Through the entire course of my treatment I'd never once cried in front of her, but now I found myself struggling to keep my composure.

"I don't know what's wrong with me. I just can't . . . I can't seem to . . ."

I would have felt like an idiot telling her that part of the problem was that I *missed* her, so I started pouring out a host of other woes instead.

"I thought everything was going to be fine once I was in remission," I quavered. "But it's been months, and I still feel so lousy. My stomach is always torn up. I can't eat. I don't have any energy. I wake up in the middle of the night, and I can't stop shaking. I've never in my life been so profoundly . . . depressed. There's something wrong with my *mind*! I can't remember my phone number sometimes. Sometimes I can't say Jerusha's name, or I'll be telling her something and the words come out all wrong. I'm not even being a good mother anymore, I'm not accomplishing anything—"

"What did you expect to accomplish other than recovery?" she asked. "This is a long process. To recover. You have been very seriously ill. You have to give yourself six months, a year even."

She sent me to a nutritionist to address the eating issue and to another gynecologist to address the symptoms of premature menopause, one of which, Gyno Man asserted, was depression. After verifying that I was no longer ovulating, he cranked up the hormone replacement therapy, replacing disobedient M. Nature with her synthetic betters. I instantly felt worse, face raging with hot flashes, body awash in night sweats. I went back, and he continued to watussi with my hormones, changing the dosage and brand names. I began to morph into something very scary almost right away. The hot flashes blazed on, migraines seized me by the skull, and I breathed fire on anyone who came within forty feet of my lair. And I gained another ten pounds.

The Gynosaur couldn't understand why I found all this so upsetting. I wasn't going to have any more children anyway, right? This was normal, he said. I'd get used to it.

"But don't the hormones increase the risk of more cancer?" I asked.

"Oh, there's some question about that," he shrugged, "but the reoccurrence rate for lymphoma is so high anyway, it doesn't make that much difference."

I went home and flushed the pills down the toilet.

Months went by. No money. No relief. No word on my manuscript. I began to wonder why I'd gone to all that trouble to survive. I visited Dr. Silverberg, but halfway through his explanation of post-traumatic stress something-or-other, I realized I was going to throw up if he didn't stop talking about it.

I spent my thirty-fourth birthday crying in the ladies room of a Chinese restaurant. One thing about chicken lo mein—it looks pretty much the same, coming or going. But throwing up brought on another hot flash, and then I had the distinct feeling I was about to see something from column B.

Gary and I drove home in silence. He no longer knew what to say.

*T*he first time I heard Fred's voice on my answering machine was just a day or two after the great lo mein birthday debacle, and I immediately recognized him as someone who was about to save my life.

"Ms. Rodgers, this is Fred Ramey with MacMurray and Beck, and we'd like to talk to you about your book . . ." I played the message over and over again, then left a message on his machine, then sat frozen to a kitchen chair until he called back two hours later.

Fred is probably used to getting the kind reception a banana gets from a howler monkey. Calling writer wannabes on the phone is as dangerous as walking over to someone in the old folk's home and saying, "How are you today?"

I'd lived in Mac and Tulsa's world off and on for almost five years by this time, and on only a few brief occasions was I able to share that world with anyone on the daily bread plane of existence. Now here was this guy who'd not only read the book—and liked it!—but he'd read it *again*, knew the characters' names, wanted to know why I'd made this or that choice for them, suggested motivations and subtleties that had honestly never occurred to me when I was writing the thing, but which all sounded terribly literary. He referred to me as an *author*, basing this assumption on my having written what was in his preeminently credible opinion, a *book*.

"What sort of advance were you hoping to receive?" he asked.

"Advance?" I squeaked. "You mean *money* in advance? Oh, I never expected you to give me an advance."

"Ah," said Fred. "Well, you . . . uh . . . you're not supposed to tell me that."

"Oh shoot!" I clapped my hand over my mouth. "You're right. What I meant to say was . . . eight million dollars. Yeah, eight million is what I usually get."

He laughed and mentioned the modest sum they were prepared to offer, and I wrote it down on a legal pad with entirely immodest circles, underlines, exclamation points, and squiggly-doodled fireworks all around it.

Fred was easy to talk to, honest but tactful. I could practically hear the leather patches on his elbows. He mentioned some of the music references in the book, which brought up the subject of his being into blues and my being into everything from Ladysmith Black Mambazo to Slim Whitman. He asked me about my family and told me about his. I smiled because he sounded just like Gary, boasting that his children were unusually smart and civilized. He mentioned he was originally from Houston but was more than pleased to not live there anymore. We were both amused to discover that we had the same little Zen calendar on our desks. But just when things started to feel more like a jam session than a job interview, the conversation took a nasty turn toward my education and credentials.

I mentioned Viterbo Fine Arts College, carefully using the term *attended* instead of *dropped out of*, then talked about growing up performing and about the radio and theater work I'd done out on the East Coast.

"And what have you been doing since you moved down to Houston?" he asked.

I thought about mentioning my agent but was afraid that that might lead to admitting she hadn't called me in seven months. I thought I might say I was writing another novel, but I suddenly remembered an old joke about two writers in a bar:

"So what have you been doing?" asks the first.

"Working on a novel," says the other.

"Yeah," the first writer sighs, "me neither."

I was torn between not wanting to sound whiny and not wanting to sound like I'd been sitting around watching the O.J. trial for the last fourteen months.

"Actually, I umm . . ." I hesitated, then opted for honesty. It takes so much less energy than schmoozing. "I've been having cancer. Chemotherapy and . . . et cetera."

This little sound bite is typically followed by a formula reaction: polite expression of sympathy, two well-meaning platitudes, tactful press for gory details.

"I see," Fred responded. "Well. Let's talk about the changes that we'd like to see in the manuscript."

"Changes?" It took me a moment to catch up. I was still in platitude-response mode.

"I should say that I was not quite caught by Mac's early pages, but with the introduction of Tulsa, the text began to flow for me. It's funny, it has a good pace. How would you feel about starting with the Tulsa material and then introducing Mac later?"

"Yes! It should. It *did*! I wrote it that way to begin with, but it kept getting rejected and—well, I was just trying to change . . . something."

"I think your first instinct was correct there. Chances are most of the people you sent it to never even looked at it, anyway.

I have to admit, when I saw the sheer bulk of it, I set it aside for quite a while myself. This is a big book you've written."

"Tell me about it," I agreed, thinking of all that paper and postage.

"So there's some significant editing to be done."

"Oh," I said. "And . . ."

"Well, this title. *Last Chance Gulch*. It just strikes me as a little Zane Gray-ish. How attached to it are you?"

"I'm not, but I don't know if I can think of a better one."

"We might do well to look at some of the song lyrics in the book and find something there. And that's another thing. Most of the lyrics have to go. Too many permissions. It gets expensive. Let the reader provide her own soundtrack."

"Okay." I was starting to feel a little overwhelmed. "Anything else?"

"Well, at times, it seems like you think everybody in the world plays the guitar."

"Everybody *does* play the guitar."

"What? No they don't."

"Sure they do. You play the guitar, don't you?"

"Well, I—yes, but—"

"There. You see?"

"Nonetheless. I was hoping we could come up with something else for the character of Aaron."

"Hmm. Maybe so. He actually started out being an artist."

"Well, here again, I think you should have gone with your first instinct."

"What else?"

"Brace yourself. This is the big one. I know this might be hard for you, but the fiction editor and I feel that the story really ends after the last scene with the Chadwicks, and everything that comes after this is sort of a movie-of-the-week wrapping up of all the details. I think you spent six hundred pages getting to one place—Mac and Tulsa together. You can't turn around and undo that in the last two chapters."

"But after he dies—that's the best writing in the book. If a person is going to cry or be affected by this book, that's where it's going to happen."

"It is well written. It's beautifully written. It's heart-breaking. But it's not part of the story. And there are higher literary goals than making people cry. These are strong characters, Joni, you have to trust that and let them go. Let the reader come to her own conclusions."

"I just feel like—if Tulsa doesn't end up on her own—if we don't see that she's okay on her own—it doesn't feel like . . . like a *circle*."

"It sounds like this is something you'll have to think about. You shouldn't change it if you don't feel it's right."

"But would you still publish the book?"

"That's something we would have to think about," he said gently.

"Fine. I'll change it."

"Well, as I said, it's something you need to think about—"

"I don't need to think about it," I cut in. "I need the damn book published. It's burning a hole in my liver. And I've got another one that's about to start burning a hole in my spleen."

"Okay, then," Fred laughed again. (Fred's an easy laugh; that's one of the things I love about him.) "What I'd like to do is send the manuscript back to you with my notes. You can decide how you want to proceed, and we'll talk."

Two days later, I got a call from an editor at the other

publisher. When I told her I was already talking with another house, she asked, "What sort of advance are they offering?"

I told her, though I wasn't sure I was supposed to. It dawned on me in that moment that this is probably why God created agents. To protect an author from editors.

"Have you signed anything yet?" she asked.

"No, but—"

"Well, don't. Let me see what we can come up with."

She thought my book was the greatest thing since toast on a stick, and she wanted to publish it with only minimal changes. My title, my ending, a guitar in every living room, and a chicken in every pot. I was elated. From beggar to chooser in less than forty-eight hours! Screw Fred Ramey and his higher literary goals. Here, at last, was someone who recognized my true brilliance!

Minutes after I hung up the phone, as if on cue, the FedEx man rang the doorbell, bringing the marked-up manuscript from MacMurray & Beck. I opened it, just to see how much red ink there really was.

There was plenty.

Virtually every page was splattered like the scene of a Civil War battle. But leafing through the carnage, I saw a better book emerging. The majority of the edits, even the small ones, served not to change, but to clarify what I was thinking, and what I was thinking was something Fred seemed to instinctively understand.

It dawned on me that this is why God created editors. To protect a book from its author.

I seized onto the editorial process for the lifeline it was, spending weeks in front of the computer and so much time on the phone that Gary began to refer to my editor as "the Ubiquitous Fred." Fred spent hours poring over the manuscript with me, explaining the terminology, procedures, and secret handshakes of the publishing industry, guiding me through each phase of production and preparing me for the next.

I argued for my original ending, but ultimately gave in to Fred's patiently immovable reasoning, and Mac and Tulsa lived happily every after.

"Trust me," he said. "I'm right. I know I'm right."

I hate to admit it, but I made the compromise because I wanted to please him. I felt I owed him something for all the time and effort he was taking to shepherd me through a process that turned out to be far more complicated than I'd anticipated. He laughed at my one-liners, told me I had an amazing sense of place. He patiently explained the hieroglyphic markings used by the copy editor and educated me on the basic elements of the business. He never acted like he was in a hurry to get off the phone, though I'm sure he often was.

I took in the powerful tonic of respect and self-respect, forced myself to eat better and go to bed early (after all, I had to *work* the next day!). I made it a goal to not let myself lie down in the afternoon, but I was usually wiped out asleep on the couch or the floor in my office when Malachi and Jerusha came home from school, anyway.

Though I still felt lousy physically, having something to *be* lifted me out of the emotional mire. It meant a great deal to me to be validated in Gary's eyes. He started feeling less like a caregiver, and I less like a burden, making us both feel more like friends again. When I got my advance, we took Malachi and Jerusha to Disney World. In their mind, it was all a wonderful gift from some mysterious benefactor. As we entered the Magic Kingdom, Jerusha proclaimed, "God bless you, Murray McBeck!"

"It's not Murray McBeck," Malachi said, rolling his eyes from a third grade pinnacle of sophistication. "It's Fred Mac-Murray."

"That's right, Ike," Gary said. "Next time you answer the phone, be sure and tell him you loved his work in *Son of Flubber.*"

"This is all very exciting," Dr. Ro acknowledged. "You see? Now everything is getting better."

"I want to thank you," I told her truly. "You saved my life. You've always been the one calm voice in all this panic, and if it wasn't for you, none of this would be happening. I would have died without ever knowing what this feels like. And it feels good. It was worth sticking around for."

"And how are you feeling? You feel well now?"

"Oh yeah, I feel great except—well, I'm really busy so, of course, my energy bank is pretty low. Sometimes if I get too tired, I run a fever in the evening. And my arms are kind of itchy again. But that's probably the humidity. . . ." As I struggled to explain away the familiar symptoms, I waited for her to jump in there and reassure me. Instead, she ordered another set of scans.

Two days later, she called me. Gary looked at me curiously from across the kitchen, seeming very far away, dark eyes asking *who is it?* I was conscious of the phone trembling in my hand. Dr. Ro never called with OK test results. That was a routine chore left to Yolanda. Dr. Ro personally delivered only the *Enola Gay* stuff.

"I will need to see you again," she said. Instead of the warm exchange that had evolved as we came to know each other, I was hearing the cool, professional voice from my first appointment. "The scans show some activity."

*T*ake a deep breath and hold it."

Red light. *Whrrrrrrrrr.*

"You may breathe."

Green light.

"Take a deep breath and hold it."

Mac and Tulsa, making love in Montana, the way Gary and I did. Still could. Will again.

"Take a deep breath and hold it."

Red light. *Whrrrrrrrrr.*

"You may breathe."

Green light.

"Take a deep breath and hold it."

My book on a shelf, in a book store. Someone reading my book on the beach, in an easy chair at home, under the fluorescent light of the public library. Jerusha would read it someday. Whatever happened, she would have that brief glimpse of who I really was. I was someone who once wrote a book.

"Take a deep breath and hold it."

Red light. *Whrrrrrrrrr.*

"You may breathe."

Green light.

"Take a deep breath and hold it."

Fred asked me one day where I'd come up with a specific image, and I confided, "I wrote it in a letter to my husband."

"You write erotic letters to your husband?"

"Now and then," I said, feeling a twinge of sadness that it was a lot more then than now.

"That's wonderful," he laughed. "You're wonderful. Everybody should know someone like you."

"Everybody *does* know someone like me. You must know at least ten of me."

"No," he said, and he wasn't laughing anymore. "There is no one like you."

Red light.

I swear I didn't mean to do it, but I had fallen completely in love. With Fred. With Mac. With the idea of seeing my book published and seeing myself as some sort of artist. I hadn't received permission to have any of these feelings. I was not allowed to like my stubby haircut or think that I was a good writer or to even imagine what it would be like to have sex with someone other than my husband. I was guilty of *thought crime*, and this was my punishment.

"Mrs. Rodgers? Hold your breath, please."

"Sorry."

I remembered Sister Maureen telling us about Etheldreda, a seventh-century Anglo-Saxon queen who wanted to be a nun instead of royalty. According to the Venerable Bede, she developed a painful tumor in her neck. "I believe that God in his goodness desires me to endure this pain in my neck," she said, "that I may be absolved from the guilt of my needless vanity. Now, instead of gold and pearls, I wear around my neck a fiery red tumor."

After her death, she was canonized as St. Audrey, and on her feast day, all the little girls wear silk chokers.

"Don't breathe, please."

"I'm sorry."

Whrrrrrrrr.

i'm sorry i'm sorry i'm sorry

Focus on *Gray's Anatomy. Encyclopaedia Britannica.* Focus on those. Cancer has nothing to do with bad thoughts, feelings, or self-indulgent artist horsecrap. The book said, "Highgrade lymphoma (nonfavorable prognosis) will reoccur in over 80% of . . ."

I went to church specifically to take Communion, beg-

ging between the lines printed in the hymnal for forgiveness
for whatever it was I was being punished for.

"Create in me a clean heart, Oh God."

"And renew a right spirit within me."

"Lift up your hearts unto the Lord."

"It is mete and right so to do."

*please god create in me a clean heart oh god I'll be good
I'll be good please*

"Take a deep breath and hold it."

Where have you been? I've been
trying to call you all week."

Fred was probably worried I was having some kind of
creative-temperament flakiness attack or something.

"Oh . . . sorry," I said. "I'm . . . I've been . . . really busy. . . ."

"How are you?"

"I'm fine," I told him, but he couldn't see my Brave Sick
Person Face over the phone.

"You don't sound fine."

"Umm . . . could I just—could I call you back, Fred?"

"No. Talk to me. Are you all right?"

Actually, I was until he asked me. I'd just completed two
perfectly businesslike phone calls in a perfectly businesslike
way. But a good editor is also a good nanny who knows how
to nurse new authors through all their histrionics. Fred, a
master mollycoddler, had created a dangerously safe haven
for me in the private confines of all that nurturing talk.

"Joni, are you all right?" he repeated.

". . . no . . ." I wished he wouldn't call me by my name.

"What's wrong?"

"I lost my remission." My voice crumpled over the words.

"Oh God . . . Joni . . . I'm sorry."

"Fred, *please*. I need to call you back later."

"No! No, you don't. I want you to talk to me."

"I don't know if I can carry on a professional conversation right now, and I really don't want to embarrass myself any worse than I already—"

"C'mon," he said, doing this very soothing thing with the timbre of his voice. "Stay with me here. This is me. It's all right."

As much as I'd been looking at *Gray's Anatomy* lately, I should have been able to locate those muscles that are supposed to keep one's chin up, but I started crying so hard, I had to press the telephone mute button so he wouldn't hear me.

"You know, I've been meaning to send you this book we did. O.T. Bonnet. *Why Healing Happens*. I'm going to send it to you along with these revisions. I don't know if you feel like reading it right now, but I'm going to send it." There was a long moment. "Are you still there?"

"Yes," I said, then remembered to unmute the phone and said "yes" again.

"Good. Don't hang up."

"Why not? I know you hate this topic."

"What do you mean?"

"Fred, we've talked on many occasions about many personal things, but every time the word *cancer* comes up, you put your mental sunglasses on."

"No, I don't."

"You do, Fred! I can tell you don't want to hear about it."

"I didn't realize I was giving you that impression," he said. "I'm sorry."

"Don't be. It's a personal matter, and this is a professional relationship."

"It's not that. It's—I guess it's just a hard subject because of . . . past experience."

"Yeah, right," I huffed, sensing the usual *once I had to have this mole removed* story coming on. "What past experience would that be?"

"My mother had cancer."

The way he said it left little doubt about the course her illness had taken.

"Oh . . . Fred . . ." I was hit by a huge hugging impulse. I was thinking of Malachi; not my baby, but the man who would someday say, "My mother had cancer" with all that shadowing in his voice and all that lead in his heart. In his absence—and Fred's—I had to draw my knees up and put my arms around them.

"It was a hard thing to watch," he said. "For a long time, I tried to hold out this Mark Twain attitude. 'I ain't got no truck with dead people.' But I thought all that was pretty well resolved. I'm sorry if—"

"No, I'm sorry," I said, the same way I hoped someone would say it to Malachi. "I've been thinking all this time you were an insensitive gnar, and in reality I was the insensitive gnar, and I'm sorry."

"What are they telling you?"

"Ro's not sure what's going on. I was feeling some symptoms, but I thought it was still from before, but I had a CAT scan, and it had changed, so I had another one, and it had grown a little more. Now I'm supposed to get another scan every four weeks so they can keep measuring it until it's big enough to biopsy."

"Why don't they biopsy it now?"

"It's right near the jugular vein. They can't just go digging around in there. Anyway, she said the bone marrow transplant—" I had to mute the phone again.

"Bone marrow transplant? That sounds like fun," Fred said, and then gave me a moment.

I cleared my throat and unmuted the phone.

"We should talk about this title, Fred. Can we just move on and make a decision on the title?"

"Okay."

There was a comforting rustle of papers in his hands. My papers. My book. As I listened to him collect it all in front of him, it made me feel a little less scattered to the wind.

"Did you make the list I asked you for?"

"Yes," I said, rifling for it in the bottom of the manuscript box. "I went to the song lyrics like you said, but I don't feel particularly enamored with any of these."

"Let's hear 'em."

"*Since My Baby Said Goodbye* . . ."

"Hmm . . . no."

". . . *Lovesick Blues* . . ."

"That is a great title—which makes me think somebody has probably used it already."

"Umm . . . *Roll with the Changes . . . I Fall to Pieces* . . ."

I read halfheartedly through the rest of the list. Most of them sounded like something a person would come up with while waiting to have blood taken by a phlebotomist. Probably because I'd compiled the list while waiting to have blood taken by the phlebotomist.

"Hmm," said Fred.

"Well, what's your suggestion?" I asked, not doubting for a moment that he had at least three.

"Have you thought about *Crazy for Trying*?"

"Oh . . . yes." I knew it was right as soon as he said it. "I mean, no—I haven't, but *yes*. From the Patsy Cline song. I can't believe I didn't think of that."

"How do you feel about it?"

"It's perfect. Because it starts with the lady on the lam

from the mental hospital and she's like this harbinger of all the insanity to come."

"It does seem that virtually every character in this book is at least slightly off balance."

"Yes," I said, making another mental apology to Mrs. Alice. "I guess they take after me."

Why Healing Happens arrived the next day.

My first impression was that Dr. O.T. Bonnet was . . . well . . . a nut. Just a few neurotransmitters short of a reticular activating formation. Compared to this guy, that coffee enema book read as sensibly as *Hints from Heloise*. But I couldn't help reading on, and though I couldn't quite buy into all of it, a lot of what he was saying started to make sense.

"We are responsible for our own well-being—our health, illnesses, and recoveries. But no individual will understand his or her relationship with health and illness without getting past the thought that guilt or blame plays a role in the process," Dr. Bonnet wrote. "To be healed, the ill must first reach inward and learn to be well again."

Skimming forward in the book, I came to a chapter entitled "On Doing Nothing."

Neither Gary nor Dr. Ro could understand why I decided not to do the CAT scans, but Ro conceded nothing terribly drastic would happen if I waited a while.

"I'm going to give myself the summer, and if it's still there, I'll do whatever she says," I promised Gary.

I was scheduled to give the commencement address at

Helena High at the end of May, and while I was there, I planned to see Sid's naturopath. I also let Kathryn, Malachi's godmother and Grandstreet's artistic director, take me to a shaman.

Fighting giggles and feeling enormously goofy about the whole scene, I arrived with Kathryn at an enormous Victorian house, a grand old structure in one of Helena's grand old neighborhoods. The house had been divided into apartments, with the shaman's home on the first floor and her—office? wigwam? plane of existence?—on the third. The shaman was a tiny woman in jean shorts and a T-shirt. It turned out I'd actually taught her two little daughters in theater school years earlier.

We drank herbal tea and talked for a while, then she instructed me to lie down in the middle of the floor on the skin of a mountain lion. She put on a CD that played a relentless drumming; electronic rhythms for the modern medicine woman. Kathryn supplemented the beat with feathered rattles, which made me feel even gigglier.

For a while, nothing happened. I just lay there, trying to swallow the Shirley MacLaine jokes that kept popping into my head.

(Knock-knock. *Who's there?* Shaman! *Shaman who?* Shaman you, you're not supposed to believe in this kind of stuff!)

I bit my lip. She murmured and twitched. After a while, she sat up and told me there were two griffins standing over me, that one of them held a ball of light in its mouth, that these were my power animals.

"Isn't it supposed to be a real animal?" I asked skeptically.

She cocked her head to the side for a moment, then reported, "They say for you, fiction is sometimes stronger than reality."

Uh huh.

She knelt over me, moaning.

"I see something that looks like the beak of a bird protruding from your neck. Here."

She sees my scar. She must have seen it. That's how she knows.

"When your spirit tries to speak, the bird gets in the way, squawking and screeching." She began to rock back and forth. Her voice rose and fell, her hands darted over my body as though she was weeding a garden. Then she sat back, her feet tucked in close to her body. "I can't do the extraction. My guide is telling me you're not ready."

Yeah, but maybe I'll be ready a hundred fifty bucks from now, right?

"There is a boy with her. . .seven or eight years old. He's so joyful." She laughed out loud. "He's riding an elephant."

The shaman lay on the lion's skin with her whole body against mine. It is difficult to speak of what happened next or what sort of time passed, because it felt for a while that I'd stepped out of the linear flow of time and was standing in one place with my past and future layered together beneath and above me the way thread spins itself around a spool. There was a profusion of sounds and images. A rushing sensation. Presences. Audiences. Blinding lights of trains and stages and operating rooms. Gary's brown-and-white wool, dark words on white pages. Malachi and Jerusha with their webby towers of cotton candy, Hannibal disappearing over the Alps with a good little girl in her St. Audrey's choker. Hurtling through my life as if it was a carnival ride, I heard the cells in my body tuning like an orchestra, all in cacophony with laughter, loss, and love.

And then I was alone with—not a vision. . .an *impression* of standing on a high, silent place. Cleansing winds came up from the badlands beneath me, lifting my arms wide, untangling my long hair from around my neck.

*T*he naturopath spent a long time talking with me, not about being sick, but about being well. This focus was the polar opposite of what I was used to, the idea that being well is not a passive state, but an active one, the idea that food equals energy, not weight.

He mentioned Dr. Andrew Weil's book *Spontaneous Healing*, agreeing with Weil's recommendations for someone with lymphoma: a clean, vegetarian diet, no caffeine, and only very limited amounts of alcohol, refined sugar, and dairy products. He also said if the September scans showed a need for additional treatment, he could offer some less-intrusive alternatives to the bone marrow transplant.

"But you did the right thing," he added. "If you'd come here with the original diagnosis, I would have told you to take the chemo. Diffuse large-cell lymphoma moves very rapidly, and you'd already advanced beyond the initial stages. However, you have a little more time now than you did then. You can make the necessary changes with the added advantage of keeping an eye on things with the CAT scans."

He prescribed medication to increase my thyroid function, along with high doses of vitamin C, a strong antioxidant compound, and echinacea and goldenseal to rebuild my immune system. To relieve the hot flashes, night sweats, and other symptoms of menopause, he recommended vitamin E, black cohash, and dong quai and encouraged me to adhere to a strict vegetarian diet with lots of soy, eliminating poultry, since anything you buy in the store is full of synthetic growth hormones, which would both exacerbate the menopause thing and pose further risk to any remission I might achieve.

Since I'd resolved not to eat red meat anymore, chicken and turkey were my main sources of protein, and I'd been eating as much as possible because the nutritionist had told me chemo erodes muscle tissue, and I would need seventy to eighty grams of protein per day to rebuild. She said once I was feeling stronger, I could drop back to forty or so grams per day, but even that was hard to do without meat. The naturopath recommended I get that same amount of protein from fish, beans, rice, tofu, and pure vegetable protein supplements instead. He also prescribed a compound called Similase, which would make it easier for me to retain and assimilate the food I was able to eat.

Back in Texas, I fasted and prayed for three days. During that time, I reread *Love, Medicine, and Miracles* by Dr. Bernie Siegel, printed out several passages, and posted them on walls, mirrors, and the refrigerator.

"One's attitude toward oneself is the single most important factor in healing or staying well."

"Cancer is a symbol, as most illness is, of something going wrong in the patient's life, a warning to him to take another road."

"When we choose to love, healing energy is released in our bodies. Energy itself is loving and intelligent and available to all of us."

I read *Healing and the Mind* by Bill Moyers, the Bible, *Black Elk Speaks*, and a new translation of the *Tao Te Ching*.

Nothing in the world
is as soft and yielding as water.
Yet for dissolving the hard and inflexible,
nothing can surpass it.
The soft overcomes the hard;
the gentle overcomes the rigid.

With my stomach bolstered by the Similase, becoming a vegetarian was no great difficulty. I had to force myself to reinstitute the process of eating, relearning to be hungry. I slowly reintroduced foods, item by item, the way a baby is introduced to rice cereal, then a smashed banana, then a little square of melba toast. Meat, chocolate, coffee, soda, and junk food in general were items I simply didn't reintroduce. It wasn't a matter of giving anything up. The effort of forcing myself to eat was significant enough that I wanted to make every morsel count.

I meditated and prayed daily. And I don't mean some pansy-ass, fold your hands and say the automatic table-grace praying. I'm talking prostrate on the floor of my office, pouring out the true contents of my heart praying, whether the true contents of my heart were penitence, gratitude, supplication, or anger. It usually started with one or all of the above and wound down to an open feeling of peace.

I embraced that peace, wanting to purify and simplify everything around me. Things over which I would have once gone ballistic now slid down my spine. I pushed aside "important" work to go swimming or read to Jerusha. I bagged out of every commitment and overcommitment I'd made, including volunteer functions and the PTO presidency. I set a strict "energy budget" and did not extend myself beyond it. Instead of fighting the afternoon naps, I planned for them, shut off the phone, and consciously gave that hour to myself each day.

My mind kept returning to all I'd seen and heard as I lay on the lion skin with the shaman's body next to mine. Struggling to integrate any of it into my traditional Judeo-Christian beliefs, I searched through the Bible, and then, unable to reach any real conclusions, gave myself permission to accept not knowing. I suspect the truth lies somewhere between Shirley MacLaine and *The 700 Club*, but I became comfortable with the idea of an open-ended "I'll ask God about it when I get there" sort of religion. I wasn't at all sure Jesus would heal me just because I asked him, but I kept asking anyway, and accepted the inner healing I found in the simple act of hanging out with him and doing my best to live whatever life I had according to his wisdom.

A strong visualized version of the Lord's Prayer became my evening meditation. I saw my book in print as I said the words "daily bread" and a dripping IV for "deliver us from evil." And "forgive us our trespasses"—well, that was Fred.

*B*ut sex in dreams almost never means sex," Silverberg said reassuringly. "It's more often a general symbol of need."

"Well, that's a relief. Because it sure seems like sex." I mulled for a moment. "That is, if I remember correctly what sex is like."

"You and your husband haven't resumed your physical relationship?"

"No. So why don't I dream about having a general symbol of need with *him*?"

"Because imaginary sex is much safer and more comfortable than a real relationship. Is it likely you'll ever become intimate with this man?"

"No! Geez . . . no. Of course not. I could never—I mean, after all Gary has done for me . . . and I love him, and—and anyway, I don't think my editor thinks of me that way. I'm positive he wouldn't if he knew what I look like right now."

"Hmm. Then it seems to me, these dreams are more about yourself."

Maybe he was right, I allowed. For a long time, the only sex I'd had was inside my head, and it was safe and comfortable to keep it there. In those disturbingly lovely dreams and daydreams, I was whole again—fully, freely, and physically alive, sacred instead of scarred, flexible instead of fragile. In the real world where Gary lived and breathed, I was battered and overweight. I hadn't forgotten the lesson I learned as an eighteen-year-old disc jockey: being invisible is more powerful than being beautiful. But Gary had seen it all. He'd been subjected to some remarkably unromantic images of me over the previous two years. I had no idea how to make myself attractive to someone who'd watched me vomit on the seat of his car, and I wasn't ready to try. We cuddled on the couch, kissed each other on the cheek and forehead, but I had no confidence in what I had to offer him anymore. The thought of his body appealed to me all right. It was the thought of *mine* that took all the fun out of it.

At the moment poor, unsuspecting Fred appeared on the scene, it was Deutschland's darkest day, and he was the best Barbarosa I could come up with. This kind friend and wise editor came into my life by the grace of God, bringing on a silver platter something I'd dreamed of since the eleventh grade. He'd restored me to the real world, educated me without making me feel ignorant, found me on unstable ground and convinced me I was solid as cedar. And all this, very gently. And I, still under the influence of passion deprivation. I knew I was way too old to be infatuated with my English teacher, and he certainly never did anything to encourage any florid fantasies, but I was smitten, and there was nothing God's army or my own lacerating guilt could do about it.

In *First, You Cry*, Betty Rollin's excruciatingly honest account of her own cancer experience, she talks about being plagued by a powerful sexual yen for her surgeon, and that made me feel a little better about being vulnerable that way. Even so, the idea I could ever feel anything for someone other than Gary hung a great purple burden of guilt around my neck, and I wasn't sure I'd ever be whole again if I couldn't unload it.

The looming prospect of the bone marrow transplant didn't make me nearly as nervous as the idea of flying to Denver to meet Fred, but going there seemed like the practical solution. Face it. Get it over with. Certainly one look at me would guarantee an absolute lack of attraction on Fred's part, and with that securely in hand, I could clear my mind of everything except the book. I wouldn't be plagued with ninth-grade study hall ponderings about if he actually thought I was wonderful or did he say that to all his authors. I could stop questioning if it was my imagination or was there actually some inexplicable, dichotomous Janis Joplin–meets–Dick Cavett chemistry between us.

Once he'd seen the real me, there would be no point in expending the effort to be clever or make him laugh or train my voice downward to the alto he'd once said he liked the sound of. (I was fireplug ugly, but my voice was still beautiful, and from the moment he made that innocent comment, I wore my vocal cords like a big ol' pair of knockers every time we spoke on the phone.)

It also occurred to me that maybe I'd luck out and he'd be some completely unattractive little pencil neck, sporting an officious three-piece suit and overly tidy power tie. Maybe the whole solicitous editor routine was a hoax, and he'd turn out to be a jerk in person. Or maybe he'd have stomach gas or halitosis or some kind of funky skin disorder. That would be perfect!

When I deplaned in Denver, Fred was standing on the concourse, eyes riveted to the wrong gate. I knew him instantly, even without the elbow patches.

Sadly, he was quite adorable.

Not in a *take me to long-term parking and ravish me, you Klingon* way, but in a slightly geeky, sweetly bookish, and uniquely Fred-like way. Wire-rim glasses circled his ocean-colored eyes, wavy hair overlapped the collar of his denim shirt. Not quite enough for a pony tail, more like a forgotten barber's appointment than a quest for lost youth. I approached him like a deer stepping into the headlights.

"Are you Fred, perchance?"

"Hi there," he smiled, and my doom was sealed.

*I*t was a productive day. Lunch with the marketing staff during which I was so nervous, I actually found myself relating some pointless anecdote about how I'd once hopped a freight in order to avoid sleeping in a Chicago Salvation Army shelter. I struggled for the rest of the time to make myself stop talking, hoping they would think I was an eccentric artist, as opposed to some blathering perimenopausal pebblehead.

Back at the office, Fred and I went over the final revisions to the manuscript (which was now officially renamed *Crazy for Trying*) and I flew one last sortie on behalf of my ending. Fred would not be moved, but he conceded on a few other issues that were in dispute, then closed the process by telling me warmly, "It's a good book."

"No it isn't," I wailed with my head in my hands. "It's the worst piece of trash ever written."

"Second worst," he comforted. "Don't forget *The Bridges of Madison County*."

At the end of the day, he drove me back to the airport, and I collapsed into a chair to wait for my flight.

The flight came and left. I stayed in the chair. Bumped.

I wasn't terribly alarmed; I'd been flying standby for

years, and I knew enough to prepare for this eventuality. I always carried a toothbrush, contact-lens solution, and a clean shirt with me and was always mentally prepared to spend another night in the airport.

The marketing director had suggested earlier that, since we didn't really have time to share our ideas, we could get together for dinner in the event I was unable to fly out as planned, so I called the office and told her I'd wait for her at the passenger-pickup area. To my horror, it was Fred's granite-colored Volvo that chugged up the ramp.

"Where's Gretchen?" I asked, squatting outside the car door.

"We decided you should come home with me. Get in."

"Oh . . . no . . . no, that's okay. Thank you, though. Really."

"What? Why not?"

"I—I don't want to inconvenience anybody or anything."

"You're not. I already talked to Edie. We'll have some dinner, and you can sleep in Anna's room. It's fine. Get in."

"No . . . no, it's not fine. She'll be pissed."

"Why do you say that?"

"Because if I were her, I'd be pissed."

"Well, you're not her, and she's not pissed. Get in the car."

Sure. Great. Terrific. I am in hell now, and I deserve it.

I stepped into the lion's mouth and buckled my seat belt.

It may seem like paradox, but most actors I know are intensely shy when confronted with the hideous prospect of playing themselves on the everyday stage of social interaction. The ride to the Ramey home was one interminable hot flash, interrupted only by periods of intense nausea.

"You know, I should really go back to the airport," I attempted, "because—see the problem is . . . well, I don't have my meds with me and—"

"There's a drugstore near my house."

"I need a prescription."

"They have a pharmacy."

"It's naturopathic."

"What is it?"

"Well, just . . . stuff . . . and some other . . . stuff . . . for my stomach."

"Well, what's it called? Maybe we can—"

"Oh, geez—*forget it*. Never mind."

"Just tell me what it is. We can try to—"

"Get off the death watch, Fred! I promise I won't keel over in front of your children, okay?"

"You said it was a problem. I'm just trying to help."

"Well, it's none of your business, so just . . . just drop it, all right?"

"Okay," he said amicably and drove on with some Fredish expression on his face.

"Your wife is going to hate me for bombing in on her like this. She'll think I'm weird. She'll think I'm horrible."

"No she won't," Fred said. "She read your book."

I wasn't jealous of Fred's wife. I may have viewed her husband as the god of all Dutch uncles and entertained a few terribly inappropriate thoughts about that lovely spot where his earlobe curved into his neck, but it was never my fantasy to live with a man whose stock-in-trade is criticizing people. I figured she must be a formidable woman.

Edie met us at the door, smiling, polite, beautiful. The slender length of her graceful dress fell the slender length of her graceful body, and she wore the innate comeliness that women spend their twenties trying to paint on, only to discover mid-thirties that it grows outward from a sharp mind, good health, and a meaningful inner life. Their home reflected the soft edges of her sensibility: unpretentious antiques, imperfect hardwood floors, old family photos in frames of silver and pewter and wood, a pleasant backyard blossoming and greening in unforced hedges and beds. The three of us sat, and as we talked a while, I saw that same soft sensibility spilling over onto Fred. She was as much the gentle architect of him as of their home. Now I wasn't sure which one of them I was in love with.

"Fred tells me you're a vegetarian," she said. "What sort of things do you eat?"

As I stammered and apologized about that, she quietly regarded me, her posture and expression unchanged.

"I'm sorry to be like this," I concluded when eye contact became too exhausting. "If it was just a matter of preference, I'd never say anything, but it's—I mean . . . honestly, I . . . I will seriously barf."

"Oh," she nodded, still unreadable except for a fleeting shadow of reaction to the word *barf*. Having grown jaded on several topics gentlefolk prefer not to discuss, I'd forgotten that blunt references to bodily functions were not as common in other households as they were in mine. She and Fred went to the kitchen, speaking in low tones. I sat in the living room, my stomach already roiling. When Fred came back, he handed me his guitar.

"I will if you will," I said, and he shrugged and went to puttering by the fireplace.

I took the guitar in my lap. My hands didn't want to do what I willed them to, but when I started singing, Fred glanced over his shoulder. I immediately lost the lyrics of the song, had to stop and fumble, then just stop.

"You have a great voice," he said.

"Well, what I lack in quality, I make up for with volume," I used my stock dodge for that compliment, handing the guitar back to him. "I'm not used to playing a six string. I just have the twelve."

"Ah." He sat on the couch with his guitar and played a brambled, bluesey riff.

"'Alberta'?" I guessed.

"Could be," he said, and started singing it in a pleasant, unaffected tenor. The effort it took to bite back the harmony radiated a physical pain from the inside of my chest, but to lay my voice across his would have felt as inappropriately intimate as a kiss on the mouth.

Fred and his jamming buddies were planning a some-what-annual gig called the Tacky Left Footer's Ball, he told me with the eagerness of a garage-band kid. Somebody was going to lower somebody else on a rope as he played the sitar on—

"Oh, you know—that Beatles song with the sitar? What is that song?"

I hate it when people assume I'm an encyclopedic fount of music trivia just because I used to be a disc jockey, and coming from Fred it always felt like the final round on *Jeopardy!*

"Umm . . . 'Love to You'?" I ventured. "Or 'Within You Without You' maybe?"

"No, no . . . it's—you know. It's that one."

The phone rang. It was one of the jamming buddies. They decided the song was in fact called "Sitar Man," and Fred relayed that to me with his hand cupped over the mouthpiece. (No mute button apparently.)

We ate dinner outside in the cool evening air; rice and vegetables, complemented by some kind of dark, heavy wine I was too bourgeois to appreciate and of which there was not nearly enough. Though I'd been avoiding alcohol, I knew my best hope, both for my stomach and for sleep, was to be half looped, but the tiny crystal glasses didn't lend themselves to much of a buzz.

Their children were unusually smart and civilized, of course. Anna was graceful and sweet, reminding me of the ballerina who lived inside the music box I still had from my seventh birthday. Parker showed me the surprisingly good drawings in his sketchbook, told me about the play he was in at school, and was the only person I actually felt comfortable talking to that entire day.

At about ten, Fred announced he was going to bed, and Edie offered me a flannel nightgown and a toothbrush. The toothbrush I gratefully accepted, remembering I'd left mine in the lav on the airplane that morning, but I couldn't bear to wear her nightgown. Even if I could have gotten it over my wide body, it would have felt sacrilegious somehow, like the hippo sporting a tutu through the celluloid frames of *Fantasia*.

Afraid I might have a night sweat in Anna's bed, I sat on the floor, leaned back against the headboard, and dozed that way for a while.

I woke up and ran to the bathroom, violently sick to my stomach, longing for my Similase. I went back to Anna's room and sat reading *The Passion of Being Woman* by Mary Hugh Scott, a pre-Fred–era MacMurray & Beck book the marketing assistant had given me on our way to lunch.

Either I copped more of a buzz than I thought, or this book was full of blinding insights. I'm too flat-chested to be a truly effective feminist (what's the point of burning your bra if you don't really need one?) but I saw in this parable of Psyche the same struggle in which I'd been engaged my whole life; the endeavor to please everyone I loved, to fulfill the expectations of everyone from Ann Landers to Frederick's of Hollywood, to fit in where I knew I didn't belong, to feel what I knew I was supposed to feel and be whom I knew I was supposed to be. But I couldn't do it. I was always getting cut from the cheerleading tryouts of life, always falling off the runway in the fashion show of societal expectation. I was never going to be the bouffant blond Never Disappoints Anyone Barbie. Ultimately, I was always going to be the bald girl in a land that worships big hair.

"Every woman in a patriarchy is in a no-win situation. If she succeeds in fitting herself into the patriarchal picture, she loses her sense of self. But if she tries to maintain her sense of self, she loses her value in the patriarchal society because she is not being an obedient woman. Either way, she faces an overwhelming sense of not being there—of not accounting for anything, not existing. . . . The terrible temptation to non-be—just to fade out . . . always hovers around her like a polluted cloud. Her oppression is the smog she must breathe every day."

It sounded like a recipe for cancer. Just add Diet Pepsi and stir.

The book began to feel heavy in my hands. I pulled on my boots and ventured out into the neighborhood.

It was a little after three-thirty, and my footsteps in the dry leaves set dogs barking behind every house I passed. Fog lay heavily over the street, but the air was clean and cold in a mountain way I tend to forget between trips to Montana. I walked until I wasn't sure where I was, then found Fred's street again, and eventually sat on his front stoop, forehead on my knees, feeling like I hadn't resolved anything. If anything, I'd made matters worse.

"*Shit*, Jesus," was the only prayer I had left. "This *hurts*."

I decided to rest for a few minutes, fetch my backpack, and hitchhike back to the airport.

*F*red came up the stairs just as I was about to walk out the door.

"Good morning," he said, though it wasn't quite morning yet, and he didn't give the impression of being much of a morning person.

"I . . . I was just getting a drink of water," I said and got one so he would see I really was.

"Well, we've got plenty of time before we have to leave. What can I get you?"

"Oh, I've got it."

"A glass of water?" he said skeptically.

"Really I'm fine. So . . . we should get there a little early, anyway. An hour . . . hour and a half. Really you can't get there too early."

I have no idea what I said on the way to the airport, but when I'm nervous, my mouth runs nonstop, so I'm sure it was an earful. I'd been going on about the rough draft of *Sugar Land* (the novel I really was working on now) and marriage and passion and women and *The Passion of Being Woman* for about half an hour when I realized Fred hadn't said anything since he pulled out of the driveway. Then I realized saying I thought *The Passion of Being Woman* is sort of a dopey title was really biting the hand that had so generously fed me, and I was instantly engulfed in another hot flash. We drove in silence until the Volvo crested a hill.

Suddenly, the sun was full round and raging orange right in front of us, just above the edge of the mountains.

The breaking of an epiphany is like the edge of orgasm. You have to stop breathing for a moment, consciously give yourself to what you unconsciously know, then accept the gift. I made a small involuntary sound, taking in the sunrise, the message, and a cleansing breath all at once.

In the moment between the sun in my eyes and my ability to look away, I saw how much energy I'd spent over the years, trying to snuff out those parts of me that were unacceptable, those glaring flaws and pesky yearnings, the messy emotions and persistent imperfections. I decided to close my eyes for a moment and, just as an experiment, give myself permission to live in my own heart.

When I opened my eyes, the sun was still raging. I had not spontaneously combusted, nor had the car disappeared off the face of the highway. The world and I were just the same, only a moment older. Fred was still sitting there beside me, and I still loved him. But the depth of my feeling for Gary was unaffected, and the lack of Fred's feeling for me was immaterial. It made no difference if what I felt was ill timed or unrequited or born out of the Passion of Being Stupid. My only fatal error would be to give in to the temptation to non-be, to inhale one more breath of the guilty black cloud.

"When we choose to love," Dr. Bernie said, "healing energy is released in our bodies."

I felt a surge of that energy as warm as the new-raging sun, knowing that only good can come from loving someone, that it is mete and right so to do. It reminded me what a double-edged decadence love is, a blessing to give and to receive. Grace. The gentle overcoming the rigid.

"I know," Fred was saying in response to the small involuntary sound. "Edie and I were on our way to a friend's cabin once, and all the sudden this huge moon was in front of us, and we both said, 'Wo! What the hell is that?'"

"Wo . . ." I echoed, and in my heart I resolved, "I gotta see more sunrises."

At the airport, Fred pulled up to the curb and looked at me expectantly.

"What," I said, "you're not even going to stir yourself out of the car to say good-bye?"

"I'm stirring," he sighed, unlatching his seatbelt.

We met by the back bumper, and I put my arms around him, just lightly, and only for a moment.

"I have an enormous crush on you," I confessed, wondering even as I said it why there's never a mute button around when you really need one.

"Do you?" He looked like he couldn't get back in his car fast enough.

"Oh yeah." I hoped he might find it gratifying on some level to know. "I think you're swell."

He might have answered, but my boots were already on their way home, and I had the good sense to stay in them.

I slept the entire flight, and when I deplaned in Houston, Gary was standing right there at the jetway. He never hangs back on the concourse with the other meeters and greeters. He's always waiting just outside the door to scoop me off the return leg of every journey, poised like a trapeze artist to catch me before I fall away again.

"Where are the kids?" I asked.

"Baby-sitter." He emphasized his intentions with amazingly dexterous eyebrows.

"In that case," I said, so very grateful to have eyebrows and intentions of my own, "take me to long-term parking and ravish me, you Klingon."

My body is the temple of the Holy Spirit. My purpose is to live. Every cell in my body is in harmony with the higher purpose of life, the superior intelligence of love. I am in remission. Remission is grace. Grace is life. Life is love. My body is the temple of the Holy Spirit. My purpose is to love.

Over the spring and summer, I drew all these things

toward me in slow tai chi movements, the sun red through my translucent eyelids, the air alive with the singing of birds. I prayed daily, taking my black cohash, dong quai, and echinacea just as religiously. The hot flashes and night sweats dissipated, and I experienced an amazing influx of energy.

He shall water his people like a garden, like a spring of water whose waters never fail. I drink deeply from that wellspring, unstopping my heart, accepting the privilege of loving.

Gary held my hand as we roamed the antique stores, feeling our own history among the memorabilia. I took Malachi and Jerusha to the pool first thing in the morning and again in the late afternoon.

Lord, you have been our dwelling place throughout all generations . . . from everlasting to everlasting, you are God . . . a thousand years are as a day in your sight. . . .

"Mom? Why are you sitting here in the dark?"

"Shush. I'm in my dwelling place."

Teach us to number our days aright that we may gain a heart of wisdom . . . satisfy us in the morning with your unfailing love. . . .

Small bursts of electricity in my brain began to recharge my efforts on the forgotten second novel. One day in early autumn, I stood up from my morning prayers to discover that my period had returned. It wasn't much—more like a comma than a period, actually. But as if it had been waiting for the allegory, the second draft of *Sugar Land* flowed out in a fresh, steady stream.

"This is a good book," I told Gary when I finished it a few weeks later.

"Cool." He was already mentally spending the advance. "What do you think your ol' buddy, Fred, will think about it?"

"Oh," I said with absolute faith, "I think he'll like it."

He didn't.

"The relationship between author and editor is an amazing thing," Carol Houk Smith, an editor at Norton, once told me. "When it works, it's wonderful. When it doesn't work, it breaks your heart."

"I'm sorry we have to come down on this side of it," Fred gently phrased the fateful phone call. "If you'd reconsider some of the changes we talked about . . ."

"Don't be sorry," I said, and I think we were both a little surprised I hadn't automatically flipped into hell-hath-no-fury mode. "I have nothing but gratitude toward MacMurray and Beck. And you, Fred. But I think this is a good book, and I don't want to apologize or compromise about it. I want it to go to someone who really loves it."

"It deserves that," he said. "You deserve that."

He told me he would push the manuscript to certain people he knew, said he still believed that someday I was going to be an author of some note, not realizing there was no need to comfort me. As much as it hurt to have the manuscript rejected by MacMurray & Beck, I was certain someone else would eventually pick it up. Maybe even a larger house with a deep pocket from which to pull some fantastically enormous advance. I was full of high hopes. I knew it was a good book. But I also knew this wasn't the right time or the right place. It felt a little like being pushed out of the nest. Like that day in Dr. Ro's office when she told me I wouldn't see her for a whole month. A terrifying prospect, but I was eager to give my wings a try.

I was ready.

Four weeks later, I returned to Dr. Ro's office.

My scans were clear.

Stop and consider! Life is but a day;
A fragile dew-drop on its perilous way.

—JOHN KEATS

*C*all me Israel.

The name means "Wrestled with God—And Won."

Right after Jacob, an Old Testament tent-dweller and infamous mama's boy, swindled his brother out of his birthright, he set out on a journey to his uncle Laban's. On the way, he had a vision of angels ascending and descending a stairway to Heaven. You'd think that would really change a person forever, especially when you consider how it inspired one of the greatest rock-and-roll anthems ever recorded, but that's not when Jacob's transformation occurred. His uncle gave him a taste of his own medicine, swindling him out of twenty-one years' labor. As a middle-aged man, Jacob was on his way home, finally prepared to face his brother again. It was then that he duked it out with God. As dawn approached, they were still locked in combat, and even though his hip had been dislocated, Jacob refused to let go until he received God's blessing.

His flaws and foibles had taken him on a long journey, and the wrestling match left him crippled, but in the end, he came away blessed and received his new name.

Israel.

Not because he was stronger than God, but because he was stronger than Jacob.

"Don't believe someone has changed when they see a vision," Michael Williams said when he told Jacob's story at a United Methodist leadership conference. "Believe it when they start acting differently."

My dad started smoking as a he-man of eleven or so. He consistently preferred elevators to stairs and was no stranger to the McAnything. His favorite meal was lots of whatever Mom was serving, folded into a well-buttered slice of white bread, forming what Gary refers to as "the Norwegian taco."

Then came the big hello. He had a heart attack.

Suddenly, life took on a whole new and much less passive meaning. He took an aggressive approach toward his own healing. He read and researched, experimented and explored. And he changed. Now, he eats, he exercises, he laughs, and he works, all with a new respect for his own life and no fear of his own death. His cardiologist loves to tell incoming patients how Del Lonnquist ran in the Governor's Cup Marathon sixteen months after his triple-bypass surgery.

My father inspired me to take charge of my own recovery. He taught me that health is something beyond the absence of disease, and life is something way beyond the absence of death. The two of us are toying with the idea of celebrating the new century by walking from Houston to Helena, and I could do it, too. At this writing, five years after a diagnosis of cancer, I'm almost as annoyingly healthy as he is.

Dr. Ro attributed my spontaneous remission to a faulty reading of the CAT scans or the fact that "lymph nodes are very reactive organs" or perhaps a belated reaction to the chemo, and she still refers to the naturopath's prescriptions as "that medicine you take for no reason." This is why I love her. I'm a highly emotional person, deeply in need of this quietly dynamic woman who keeps me grounded in the scientific aspect of this psychological lollapalooza.

At first, I measured my remission in inches. I started out with an Annie Lennox flattop, progressed to a Dorothy Hammel wedge, then a Marlo Thomas flip-do. But just as I was regaining my Fabio flow, I decided my time was too precious to spend with a blow dryer, and I've worn a boyish razor cut ever since.

Jerusha says the scar left on my arm by the longline looks a bit like a thunderbird. Or a phoenix. The scar on my neck makes me feel sort of cocky. Like a biker girl. Tough chick. I've grown used to seeing someone different in the mirror. Sometimes, as I stand combing out my short shock of hair or smoothing vitamin E moisturizer into the lines around my eyes and the bower around my breast, just for a moment sometimes, I even think I'm beautiful. I still see Grampa Emil there, but now a taller, somewhat zaftig version of my mother has joined him, along with shades of Janis and Jerusha and Lillian Isabel. There's even a bit of old Twelve Toes about my high cheekbones—or maybe it's the scars—but it all comes together in a sort of Pioneer Woman of Suburbia look.

Badlands Barbie.

I still follow a clean nutritional regimen, slipping up just often enough to avoid being obnoxious about it. I don't drink alcohol or soda. I never eat any kind of meat, poultry, or chocolate and do my best to avoid processed flour and sugar. (This is also great for Gary; since sex is the only vice I

have left, I have to make the most of it.) It's not that I think
one chocolate bar or half a glass of wine will kill me, but the
journey of a thousand miles begins with a single step—and so
does the journey backward.

I ordered the latest round of Richard Simmons tapes and
found that I could even stomach the ab work. My friend Gay
Lynn and I made a pact to meet on the corner every morning
at six and go for a brisk three-mile walk with our dogs. After
two years of diehard doing it, I'm in much better shape, and
my dog isn't nearly as apt to swipe and destroy socks from
the laundry hamper. I'm not exactly svelte, but the numbers
no longer determine how I feel about myself. In fact, I only
weigh myself once every six months at Dr. Ro's office. I'm no
longer at war with my body. I feed it and move it and allow it
to rest. In return, it takes me through each day, reminding me
that my energy is precious and that I must also feed and rest
and exercise my soul. I'm no longer willing to devote energy
to pretending to like Mahler when I actually like Midler, but
I try not to skimp on letting the people I love know how
important they are. Daily prayer and meditation are still my
spiritual antioxidants, and I try to keep my body and spirit as
junk free as possible.

Crazy for Trying was released in November 1996. Of
course, my head expanded dangerously with First Novel Syndrome, and I took it all way too seriously right up until I, my
parents, and the bookstore owner were the only ones at my
first book signing. After that, reality was checked and a fairly
even keel retained. Thanks to the efforts of the MacMurray
& Beck staff, the book was selected to be featured in the
Barnes & Noble Discover Great New Writers program and
was a finalist for the Discover Award. It received universally
glowing reviews—well, from the *good* reviewers, anyway. I
don't count that snavely miscreant who obviously suffers

from the literary equivalent of penis envy or the no-forehead cretin who just plain didn't get it.

Happily, enough of the reading public liked it that Gary and I were able to buy a house. We made the down payment with my first royalty check, prompting Gary to dub our residence "the House That Mac Built." He has a garden and pecan trees, Malachi and Jerusha have a puppy named Redbone, and I am in the process of painting every stark white wall with the boldest colors I can find in cans. It feels good to be home.

Since I've journeyed on to other publishers, I seldom see or hear from Fred, but bound by the ancient tradition that decrees you are forever a slave to the one who saves your life, I tend to obsess over whether he's read my current book or article and whether it meets his approval. I'm certain he doesn't think of me nearly as often or as fondly as I think of him. I suspect I'm like a little mosquito he's too kind to swat, buzzing occasionally past the periphery of his thoughts with thinly annoying reminders of certain things that both pleasure and plague him, things he simultaneously loves and hates—self-indulgent writer horsecrap, the Houston he thought he could leave behind, Little Zen Calendars, and a mommy with cancer.

Sugar Land was eventually released by Spinsters Ink, a wonderfully courageous feminist publisher, and again I was blessed with an intuitive, nurturing editor. If Fred Ramey introduced me to the art of fiction, Joanie Drury introduced me to the craft. No one is more surprised than I am to arrive at this chapter and discover I turned out to be a writer.

"What will you do next?" Gary asked as we lay together looking at my name in the "Book Events" section of the Sunday *Chronicle*. "Hey, why don't you do something with car chases? Or something with the Russian army coming over the hill. Do something where the Russian army comes over the hill and gets into a car chase."

"Actually," I tried to tell him gently, "I think I'm going to write a book about cancer."

"Oh, geez. Do you really have to?"

"I'm sorry, Gar Bear. I think I really do."

"Do I have to be in it?"

"Every day."

"All right," he looked at me with one eyebrow crinkled inward, "but only if you change my name to Rueben and make me a babe magnet."

I laughed and shifted my shoulder into the crook of his arm.

"So," he asked, wrapping around me like a warm winter coat, "how does it end?"

I considered it carefully, then answered, "I live."

I am writing this in my office, my favorite room in the house. The walls are soft ocher, filled with images from the Louvre, Montana, and my children's art classes, but I have my two favorite pictures perched on a shelf not far from the healing mandala made of my braids.

In the first picture, I'm healthy and strong, and I have beautiful, long hair. It's Jerusha's birthday, and I'm holding her in my arms, and we're laughing. In the second photo, I'm sick and weak, and my beautiful long hair is long gone. But I'm holding Jerusha in my arms, and we are laughing.

These two moments seemed so far apart at the time, but now they stand together side by side, like thread wrapped around a spool, reminding me what a joyful and hilarious thing life is, even when it has a little cancer in it. If I lose that joy, I lose my incentive to survive. I suppose it's possible to live without laughing—but what would be the point?

When I was sick, someone sent me a little wooden plaque that said, "Adversity is a blessing." But I disagree. The overcoming of adversity is a blessing. The comfort, strength, and love that manifest themselves in times of adversity are a blessing. Adversity is not a blessing. Adversity just sucks. Although I'm grateful for the grace and the growing I found, I will never say I'm glad I had cancer. Perhaps I could have grown as much without it by listening to my parents, cherishing my marriage, being with my children, building my career. Would to God I'd had that chance.

"Cancer is the definition of who I am now," said one survivor in a magazine article I read a while back. But if cancer is what we are, and all our efforts are bent toward killing cancer, then what's to become of us?

Cancer is not what I am. It's not a gift or a curse. It's not a blessing in disguise (unless that is one *dang* good disguise!). It's not the scourge of God, not the Red Badge of Courage, nor is it a purely clinical phenomenon. Personally, I like Malachi's definition: "Cancer is what happens when your cells decide to go funky." We are who we are, regardless of a few funky cells, and surviving cancer is the same as emerging from any of life's refining fires. It combines the two powerful elements of that famous sports show intro—the thrill of victory and the agony of defeat—all wrapped up in one swift kick in the head.

I'm still wondering if and when I'll ever "get over it." After all this time, cancer can still reach out and grab me with insidious tentacles of survivor's guilt, fears of reoccurrence, self-pitying fantasies of what might have been had the beast passed me by, and worst of all, nostalgic thoughts of how lovely it was when I was being nurtured and fussed over and praised for my courage and strength.

When Jerusha was about four, I had occasion to scold at her, "You need to know, Missy, this entire world does not revolve around you."

"I know," she answered with a child's honesty. "That's what I hate about it!"

If I were to be equally honest, I'd have to admit I liked having people fuss and fawn over me. What fun, sporting a better excuse and a bigger scar than anyone else in the room, being the focus of my parents' concern, enjoying daily, graphic demonstrations of how much my husband valued and cherished me (especially after *years* of trying to impress upon him how I was the only light in his otherwise meaningless existence!). These were seductive elements for a melodrama junkie like me. Growing up, I was just number five of six. More than anything, I wanted to be something different, something special. When I had cancer, I was the center of my family's attention. Just what I'd always wanted. But how much better it is to be nurtured out of unconditional love, to be praised for accomplishments, or even be out and out ignored by the world but satisfied within one's self.

We learn early that it's *fun* to be sick, associating it more with Popsicles, ginger ale, and a day off from school more than with pain, diarrhea, or death. These are powerful subliminal messages. I'm a nurturing and caring mother when one of my children is sick, but between the back rubs and solicitude, I make it a point to pay additional attention to the well child, too. I treat the well child to something special and, though this may sound cruel, I make sure it's something the sick child will be madly envious of. Gary and I also allow a few "mental health days" off from school every year, eliminating both the unconscious desire to be sick and the need for them to feign sickness in order to get the little break everybody needs once in a while. Now, when I'm holding Malachi's head while he vomits through some flu bug, I don't stroke his neck and murmur, "It's okay." I stroke his neck and murmur, "Man, being sick is no fun, is it?"

Like any of life's refining fires, cancer is a potentially profound learning experience. So what did I learn?

I learned that profound learning experiences are vastly overrated.

And I learned nose hair is there for a reason.

And I learned . . . oh, yeah—straw hats go with everything.

I pretend no other wisdom than this.

I don't advocate chemo, though I believe it's the reason I'm alive today. I don't recommend being a vegetarian, though I believe it's the reason I'll still be alive in twenty years (but I could be crossing the street tomorrow and get hit by a bus!) I don't endorse any of the books mentioned here, though I've read them ragged and refer to them often, and I don't suggest you consult with a naturopath or nutritionist or shaman or shrink.

I advocate life. I recommend joy. I endorse forgiveness, and I suggest you seek until you find whatever it is you need, be it straight allopathic medicine, alternative methods, or mulligan stew. Because the oncologist and everyone else from priests to pathologists—they're just Ground Control. You're Major Tom.

If cancer is part of your journey, you are daily in my circle of prayers, but it wasn't my intention to spout pink politics or a religious manifesto here. This book is not intended to be a Bible or a battle plan or chicken soup for anyone's soul. (Chicken is laden with artificial estrogens, anyway. Most souls I know would be better served by a Harvey Wallbanger.) I wouldn't presume to offer medical advice, and I didn't set out to inspire or scare you with the terrible tale of how my body rebelled and my hair fell out. I just wanted to tell you my story, because I wanted to tell you this: It does grow back.

One way or another, all things come to their healing.

Truly, I promise you, grace is real, God is here, and in the end, everything is going to be all right.

362.196 Rodgers, Joni
R

Bald in the land
of big hair